Lecture Notes
in Business Information Processing   499

Series Editors

Wil van der Aalst ⓘ, *RWTH Aachen University, Aachen, Germany*
Sudha Ram ⓘ, *University of Arizona, Tucson, AZ, USA*
Michael Rosemann ⓘ, *Queensland University of Technology, Brisbane, QLD, Australia*
Clemens Szyperski, *Microsoft Research, Redmond, WA, USA*
Giancarlo Guizzardi ⓘ, *University of Twente, Enschede, The Netherlands*

LNBIP reports state-of-the-art results in areas related to business information systems and industrial application software development – timely, at a high level, and in both printed and electronic form.

The type of material published includes

- Proceedings (published in time for the respective event)
- Postproceedings (consisting of thoroughly revised and/or extended final papers)
- Other edited monographs (such as, for example, project reports or invited volumes)
- Tutorials (coherently integrated collections of lectures given at advanced courses, seminars, schools, etc.)
- Award-winning or exceptional theses

LNBIP is abstracted/indexed in DBLP, EI and Scopus. LNBIP volumes are also submitted for the inclusion in ISI Proceedings.

Aleksander Jarzębowicz · Ivan Luković ·
Adam Przybyłek · Mirosław Staroń ·
Muhammad Ovais Ahmad · Mirosław Ochodek
Editors

Software, System, and Service Engineering

S3E 2023 Topical Area, 24th Conference on Practical Aspects
of and Solutions for Software Engineering, KKIO 2023
and 8th Workshop on Advances in Programming Languages, WAPL 2023
Held as Part of FedCSIS 2023, Warsaw, Poland, 17–20 September 2023
Revised Selected Papers

Springer

Editors
Aleksander Jarzębowicz (iD)
Gdańsk University of Technology
Gdansk, Poland

Ivan Luković (iD)
University of Belgrade
Belgrade, Serbia

Adam Przybyłek (iD)
Gdańsk University of Technology
Gdańsk, Poland

Mirosław Staroń (iD)
University of Gothenburg
Gothenburg, Sweden

Muhammad Ovais Ahmad (iD)
Karlstad University
Karlstad, Sweden

Mirosław Ochodek (iD)
Poznan University of Technology
Poznan, Poland

ISSN 1865-1348   ISSN 1865-1356 (electronic)
Lecture Notes in Business Information Processing
ISBN 978-3-031-51074-8   ISBN 978-3-031-51075-5 (eBook)
https://doi.org/10.1007/978-3-031-51075-5

This Springer imprint is published by the registered company Springer Nature Switzerland AG
The registered company address is: Gewerbestrasse 11, 6330 Cham, Switzerland

Paper in this product is recyclable.

Preface

In today's digital age, software is the backbone of every aspect of our lives, from the applications on our smartphones to the systems that drive industries, healthcare, and entertainment. Software engineers are the architects and builders of this digital realm, shaping the future with their code. Their work is informed by the methods, techniques, and approaches put forth by researchers, who are at the forefront of innovation, continuously pushing the boundaries of what is possible in a rapidly evolving landscape. The gathering of these minds to share their insights, discoveries, and experiences is of paramount importance.

For decades, Conference on Practical Aspects of and Solutions for Software Engineering (KKIO) and Workshop on Advances in Programming Languages (WAPL) have served as platforms for the exchange of knowledge, fostering collaboration and sparking new ideas that drive the industry forward. In 2023, these two esteemed events were coordinated under the umbrella of Software, System, and Service Engineering (S3E), which, in turn, formed an integral part of the FedCSIS conference. The conference was held in Warsaw, Poland, from September 17 to 20, 2023.

In total, our three research events attracted 55 submissions. After a rigorous single-blind peer-review process, which included at least 3 reviews per submission, 9 were accepted as full papers, 3 as short papers, 1 as a keynote paper, 3 as communication papers, and 2 as position papers (the details regarding the acceptance of submissions at each event are presented in Table 1; enclosed in parentheses is the number of papers chosen for inclusion in this monograph). The accepted papers were presented to a well-focused audience, fostering discussions that not only enriched the authors but also illuminated novel directions for future research endeavors. Following the events, the authors of 6 papers presented during the conference were invited to submit revised and extended versions of their work for inclusion in this post-conference monograph.

Table 1. Counts of accepted and rejected submissions. Enclosed in parentheses is the number of papers chosen for inclusion in this monograph.

	KKIO	S3E	WAPL
Full papers	6 (3)	2 (1)	1 (1)
Short papers	3 (1)		
Keynote papers	1		
Communication papers		3	
Position papers	1		1
Rejected submissions	30	7	
Total	**41**	**12**	**2**

We extend our heartfelt gratitude to all who contributed to the success of our research events. We begin by thanking the authors for their invaluable contributions, the attendees whose active participation fueled fruitful discussions, and the dedicated members of the Program Committees who invested their time and effort in providing insightful feedback. Furthermore, we wish to express our appreciation to the chairs of the FedCSIS conference series, namely Maria Ganzha, Leszek Maciaszek, Marcin Paprzycki, and Dominik Ślęzak, as well as Paweł, Szmeja and Piotr Sowiński who promptly handled our technical requests, for their valuable assistance in organizing our events. Additionally, our sincere thanks go to the team at Springer, for their instrumental role in bringing this volume to life. Lastly, we acknowledge Muhammad Ovais Ahmad and Mirosław Ochodek for their assistance in soliciting papers, writing missing reviews, and balancing reviews at KKIO 2023. Although they were not program chairs, their contributions were significant, leading us to include them as co-editors of the post-proceedings.

We trust that you will find this monograph to be a valuable resource for your professional and academic pursuits, and we wish you an engaging read. We also extend a warm invitation to visit our event websites at https://kkio.pti.org.pl/2024 and https://2024.fedcsis.org/main/s3e to join us for upcoming editions.

November 2023

Aleksander Jarzębowicz
Ivan Luković
Adam Przybyłek
Mirosław Staroń
Muhammad Ovais Ahmad
Mirosław Ochodek

Organization

KKIO 2023

Program Committee Chairs

Aleksander Jarzębowicz   Gdańsk University of Technology, Poland
Adam Przybyłek   Gdańsk University of Technology, Poland
Mirosław Staroń   University of Gothenburg, Sweden

Steering Committee

Marek Bolanowski	Rzeszow University of Technology, Poland
Bogumiła Hnatkowska	Wrocław University of Science and Technology, Poland
Stanisław Jarząbek	Białystok University of Technology, Poland
Sylwia Kopczyńska	Poznań University of Technology, Poland
Piotr Kosiuczenko	Military University of Technology in Warsaw, Poland
Lech Madeyski	Wrocław University of Science and Technology, Poland
Mirosław Ochodek	Poznań University of Technology, Poland
Aneta Poniszewska-Maranda	Lódz University of Technology, Poland
Michał Śmialek	Warsaw University of Technology, Poland
Bartosz Walter	Poznań University of Technology, Poland

Program Committee

Muhammad Ovais Ahmad	Karlstad University, Sweden
Mohammad Alshayeb	King Fahd University of Petroleum and Minerals, Saudi Arabia
Shariq Aziz Butt	University of Lahore, Pakistan
Ilona Bluemke	Warsaw University of Technology, Poland
Tomasz Boiński	Gdańsk University of Technology, Poland
Marek Bolanowski	Rzeszow University of Technology, Poland
Leszek Borzemski	Wrocław University of Science and Technology, Poland
Alena Buchalcevova	Prague University of Economics and Business, Czech Republic

Matteo Camilli	Politecnico di Milano, Italy
Stanislav Chren	Aalto University, Finland
Wiktor Bohdan Daszczuk	Warsaw University of Technology, Poland
Włodzimierz Dąbrowski	Warsaw University of Technology, Poland
Anna Derezinska	Warsaw University of Technology, Poland
Remy Dupas	Université de Bordeaux, France
Arpita Dutta	National University of Singapore, Singapore
Mariusz Flasiński	Jagiellonian University, Poland
Mouzhi Ge	Deggendorf Institute of Technology, Germany
Denys Gobov	National Technical University of Ukraine Kyiv Polytechnic Institute, Ukraine
Krzysztof Goczyła	Gdańsk University of Technology, Poland
Paweł Góra	University of Warsaw, Poland
Jere Grönman	Tampere University, Finland
Karthick Gunasekaran	University of Massachusetts, USA
Piotr Habela	Polish-Japanese Academy of Information Technology, Poland
Dávid Halász	Masaryk University, Czech Republic
Ridewaan Hanslo	University of Pretoria, South Africa
Sebastian Heil	Chemnitz University of Technology, Germany
Sebastian Herold	Karlstad University, Sweden
Bogumiła Hnatkowska	Wrocław University of Science and Technology, Poland
Philipp Hohl	ZF Friedrichshafen AG, Germany
Zbigniew Huzar	Wrocław University of Science and Technology, Poland
Irum Inayat	National University of Computer and Emerging Sciences, Pakistan
Stanisław Jarząbek	Białystok University of Technology, Poland
Frank Johnsen	Norwegian Defence Research Establishment, Norway
Marija Katić	Birkbeck, University of London, UK
Wiem Khlif	University of Sfax, Tunisia
Barbara Kitchenham	Keele University, UK
Sylwia Kopczyńska	Poznań University of Technology, Poland
Piotr Kosiuczenko	Military University of Technology, Poland
Marek Krętowski	Białystok University of Technology, Poland
Martin Kropp	University of Applied Sciences and Arts Northwestern Switzerland, Switzerland
Kevin Lano	King's College London, UK
Maria Lencastre	Escola Politécnica de Pernambuco - UPE, Brazil
Rafał Leszczyna	Gdańsk University of Technology, Poland

Tomasz Lewowski — Wrocław University of Science and Technology, Poland

Ilaria Lunesu — Università degli Studi di Cagliari, Italy

Lech Madeyski — Wrocław University of Science and Technology, Poland

Bartosz Marcinkowski — University of Gdańsk, Poland

Christoph Matthies — Hasso Plattner Institute at the University of Potsdam, Germany

Jacek Maślankowski — University of Gdańsk, Poland

Jakub Miler — Gdańsk University of Technology, Poland

Durga Prasad Mohapatra — NIT Rourkela, India

Jerzy Nawrocki — Poznań University of Technology, Poland

Ērika Nazaruka — Riga Technical University, Latvia

Michael Neumann — Hochschule Hannover, Germany

Yen Ying Ng — Nicolaus Copernicus University, Poland

Arne Noyer — Ostfalia University of Applied Sciences, Germany

Mirosław Ochodek — Poznań University of Technology, Poland

Necmettin Özkan — Kuveyt Türk Participation Bank, Turkey

Mel Ó Cinnéide — University College Dublin, Ireland

Subhrakanta Panda — Birla Institute of Technology and Science, Pilani, India

Andrzej Paszkiewicz — Rzeszow University of Technology, Poland

Rui Humberto R. Pereira — Instituto Politécnico do Porto - ISCAP, Portugal

Aneta Poniszewska-Marańda — Łódź University of Technology, Poland

Michał Przybyłek — Polish-Japanese Academy of Information Technology, Poland

Łukasz Radliński — West Pomeranian University of Technology, Poland

Petri Rantanen — Tampere University, Finland

Sonja Ristić — University of Novi Sad, Serbia

Adam Roman — Jagiellonian University, Poland

Bruno Rossi — Masaryk University, Czech Republic

Mika Saari — Tampere University, Finland

Małgorzata Sadowska — Wrocław University of Science and Technology, Poland

Sławomir Samolej — Rzeszow University of Technology, Poland

Eva-Maria Schön — University of Applied Sciences Emden/Leer, Germany

Marcin Sikorski — Gdańsk University of Technology, Poland

Gheorghe Cosmin Silaghi — Babeş-Bolyai University, Romania

Zipani Tom Sinkala — Karlstad University, Sweden

Michel Soares — Federal University of Sergipe, Brazil

Janusz Sosnowski — Warsaw University of Technology, Poland

Zenon Sosnowski	Białystok University of Technology, Poland
Andrzej Stasiak	Military University of Technology, Poland
Krzysztof Stencel	University of Warsaw, Poland
Jacek Stój	Silesian University of Technology, Poland
Jakub Swacha	University of Szczecin, Poland
Tomasz Szmuc	AGH University of Science and Technology, Poland
Marcin Szpyrka	AGH University of Science and Technology, Poland
Mariusz Szwoch	Gdańsk University of Technology, Poland
Michał Śmiałek	Warsaw University of Technology, Poland
Adam Trendowicz	Fraunhofer IESE, Germany
Bartosz Trybus	Rzeszow University of Technology, Poland
Dimitri Van Landuyt	Catholic University of Leuven, Belgium
José Luis Vázquez-Poletti	Complutense University of Madrid, Spain
Anita Walkowiak-Gall	Wrocław University of Science and Technology, Poland
Wojciech Waloszek	Gdańsk University of Technology, Poland
Bartosz Walter	Poznań University of Technology, Poland
Andrzej Wardziński	Gdańsk University of Technology, Poland
Shakthi Weerasinghe	Deakin University, Australia
Jan Werewka	AGH University of Science and Technology, Poland
Bogdan Wiszniewski	Gdańsk University of Technology, Poland
Krzysztof Wnuk	Blekinge Institute of Technology, Sweden
Konrad Wrona	NATO Communications and Information Agency, The Netherlands
Krzysztof Wyrzykowski	NET PC, Poland
Andrzej Zalewski	Warsaw University of Technology, Poland
Janusz Zalewski	Florida Gulf Coast University, USA
Teresa Zawadzka	Gdańsk University of Technology, Poland
Hongyu Zhang	University of Newcastle, Australia
Zbigniew Zieliński	Military University of Technology, Poland

S3E 2023

Program Committee Chairs

Ivan Luković	University of Belgrade, Serbia
Aleksandar Popović	University of Montenegro, Montenegro
Ayça Kolukısa Tarhan	Hacettepe University, Turkey
Marjan Mernik	University of Maribor, Slovenia

Program Committee

Muhammad Ovais Ahmad	Karlstad University, Sweden
Srdja Bjeladinovic	Faculty of Organizational Sciences, University of Belgrade, Serbia
Anna Derezinska	Institute of Computer Science, Warsaw University of Technology, Poland
Vladimir Dimitrieski	Faculty of Technical Sciences, Serbia
Arpita Dutta	National University of Singapore, Singapore
Ferhat Erata	Yale University, USA
M. J. Escalona	University of Seville, Spain
Hamido Fujita	Iwate Prefectural University, Japan
Gabriel García-Mireles	Universidad de Sonora, Mexico
Arda Göknil	SINTEF Digital, Norway
Ridewaan Hanslo	University of Pretoria, South Africa
Sebastian Heil	Technische Universität Chemnitz, Germany
Kalinka Kaloyanova	University of Sofia, Bulgaria
Marija Katic	University of London, UK
Wiem Khlif	FSEGS, Tunisia
Nenad Krdzavac	University of Belgrade, Serbia, Serbia
Bartosz Marcinkowski	University of Gdansk, Poland
Boris Milašinović	Faculty of Electrical Engineering, University of Zagreb, Croatia, Croatia
Gordana Milosavljevic	Faculty of Technical Sciences, Serbia
Sanjay Misra	Østfold University, Norway
Miguel Ehécatl Morales Trujillo	University of Canterbury, New Zealand
Necmettin Ozkan	Kuveyt Turk Participation Bank, Turkey
Mert Ozkaya	Yeditepe University, Turkey
Sonja Ristic	University of Novi Sad, Faculty of Technical Sciences, Serbia
Bruno Rossi	Masaryk University, Czech Republic
Milan Segedinac	Faculty of Technical Sciences, Novi Sad, Serbia
Jose Luis Sierra	Universidad Complutense de Madrid, Spain
Maria João Varanda Pereira	Instituto Politécnico de Bragança, Portugal
Vassilios Vescoukis	National Technical University of Athens, Greece

WAPL 2023

Program Committee Chairs

Jan Janousek	Czech Technical University, Czech Republic
Ivan Luković	University of Belgrade, Serbia
Marjan Mernik	University of Maribor, Slovenia
Boštjan Slivnik	University of Ljubljana, Slovenia
Pedro Rangel Henriques	Universidade do Minho, Portugal
Maria Joao Varanda Pereira	Instituto Politecnico de Braganca, Portugal
Geylani Kardas	Ege University, Turkey

Program Committee

Önder Babur	Eindhoven University of Technology, Netherlands
Ankica Barisic	Université Côte d'Azur, Croatia
Darius Blasband	RainCode, Belgium
Zoltán Horváth	Eotvos Lorand University, Budapest, Hungary
Jan Janousek	Czech Technical University Prague, Czechia
Paul Keir	University of the West of Scotland, UK
Tomaz Kosar	University of Maribor, Slovenia
Pablo E. Martínez López	Universidad Nacional de Quilmes, Argentina
Marjan Mernik	University of Maribor, Slovenia
Boris Milašinović	Faculty of Electrical Engineering, University of Zagreb, Croatia, Croatia
Mert Ozkaya	Yeditepe University, Turkey
Nikolaos Papaspyrou	National Technical University of Athens, Greece
Jaroslav Porubän	Technical University of Košice, Slovakia
Pedro Rangel Henriques	University of Minho, Portugal
João Saraiva	University of Minho, Portugal
Jose Luis Sierra	Universidad Complutense de Madrid, Spain
Jeremy Singer	University of Glasgow, UK
Bostjan Slivnik	University of Ljubljana, Slovenia
Hasan Sozer	Ozyegin University, Turkey
Maria João Varanda Pereira	Instituto Politécnico de Bragança, Portugal
Jan Vitek	Northeastern University, USA
Vadim Zaytsev	Universiteit Twente, Netherlands

Contents

24th Conference on Practical Aspects of and Solutions for Software Engineering (KKIO 2023)

A Proposal for Functional Software Identification Using Risk-Based Continuous Quality Control

Levin Chee Xian Ho[1,2(✉)], Marko Esche[1], Martin Nischwitz[1,2],
Reinhard Meyer[1], and Sabine Glesner[2]

[1] Physikalisch-Technische Bundesanstalt, Berlin, Germany
{levin.ho,marko.esche,martin.nischwitz,reinhard.meyer}@ptb.de
[2] Technical University of Berlin, Berlin, Germany
sabine.glesner@tu-berlin.de

Abstract. Software environments have become increasingly sophisticated in recent years, giving rise to modern measuring instruments that use simple hardware sensors but defined with complex software. The conformity of such devices in the legally regulated sector is usually ensured by using version numbers or hashes over executable binaries, which is inefficient due to the sensitivity of hashes to even small changes in the code. However, the legal requirements could also be equally satisfied if the certified prototype and devices in field possess identical functional behavior, even when hashes differ. With such functional identification, the device manufacturers could gain the opportunity to introduce software patches or bugfixes without having to go through the complete mandatory certification process again. Based on the L^* algorithm, which learns the accepted language and hence the internal state model of the instrument software represented by deterministic finite automata, a risk-based method is proposed to realize automatic functional identification of software to a certain extent, thereby allowing continuous quality control of periodically updated measuring instruments without frequent manual certifications. Risk assessment is used to identify critical modifications introduced in monitored devices, which then triggers warnings for manual inspections when necessary. This article is an extended version of the work previously published in [7] and is envisioned to be a first step to realize fully automatic quality control for regulated measuring instruments.

Keywords: Risk assessment · Functional identification · Automatic quality control · Automata learning · Legal metrology

1 Introduction

Modern communication infrastructure and the ubiquitous availability of significant computational power even in small devices such as smart sensors allow

© The Author(s), under exclusive license to Springer Nature Switzerland AG 2024
A. Jarzębowicz et al. (Eds.): KKIO 2023, LNBIP 499, pp. 3–34, 2024.
https://doi.org/10.1007/978-3-031-51075-5_1

software developers to remotely and regularly fix bugs identified during use of an IT component in the field. The same mechanism can also be used to deliver upgraded software frequently to remote devices to fulfill customer's needs, enabling IT equipment manufacturers to sell devices equipped with long-living hardware. However, this development also comes at a certain cost: The capabilities of remote updates have proven to introduce unexpected or unintended errors into otherwise stable systems [10]. Therefore, approaches to cover this gap (without forcing potential users of updated software to validate the complete software of a device) have received significant attention in various publications [13,18]. Such approaches enable users of IT equipment to monitor a device's behavior for potential anomalies without having to verify each individual update, thus providing a high-level approach to identify software by means of its functionality rather than by means of its binary pattern.

Monitoring and identifying a device's functional behaviour becomes especially important if requirements on these devices are mandated by legal regulations, typically involving recertification of the entire system in case of modifications. One industry sector affected by such regulations is Legal Metrology covering measuring instruments placed on the market in the European Union for commercial or official use. These regulated instruments include, e.g., taximeters for taxi fare calculation, gas meters for measuring gas consumption and length measuring instruments to measure the dimensions of sold products. Any of these instrument put on the common EU market has to be subjected to a conformity assessment according to Annex II of the Measuring Instruments Directive 2014/32/EU (MID) [4]. A notified body performing this task is, for instance, Germany's national metrology institute, namely the Physikalisch-Technische Bundesanstalt (PTB).

During conformity assessment, manufacturers have to demonstrate that their instrument fulfills the essential requirements given in Annex I of the MID. During use, market surveillance authorities across the EU monitor these devices and their usage to detect any potential non-compliance. As an example, essential requirement 8.3 states that, "Software that is critical for metrological characteristics shall be identified as such and shall be secured. Software identification shall be easily provided by the measuring instrument. Evidence of an intervention shall be available for a reasonable period of time." [4]. This entails the identifiability of software in general, and beyond the possibility to detect changes to said software and makes them evident to all parties involved. Typically, both identifiability and detection of changes are achieved by using cryptographic hashes over the executable binaries to identify specific versions of the software and to detect any unwanted modifications [2]. However, such an approach quickly may put serious strain onto the conformity assessment bodies and market surveillance authorities. For example, even recompilation of an otherwise unchanged source code may result in a different hash value due to the inclusion of compiled time stamps. Therefore, solutions that automatically evaluate software modifications on a higher level and link them to a potential risk of non-compliance are needed.

From this point of view, the ability to perform accurate functional identification onto software subjected to legal control may significantly reduce the effort needed to monitor and to detect unwanted modifications in said software by conformity assessment bodies or market surveillance authorities. In brief, functional identification is defined as a methodology that seeks to ensure the consistency and the essential functional behavior of a certain software as per defined software requirements [17]. Usually, functional identification is performed by treating software as a black-box, that is, evaluating the software compliance by functional behavior without knowing the internal structure of the software, thus allowing a reduced confirmation bias compared to manual identification such as comparing cryptographic hashes [17]. For identifying modifications in software - as in this article - functional identification can be performed via several steps: learning the functional behavior of a certified software (before modification); verifying the modified software based on the previously learned functional behavior; updating learned functional behavior (if the implemented modification is accepted) or triggering a manual recertification while retaining original functional behavior (if a critical behavioral change of software function is detected). Hence, functional identification potentially allows easier detection of non-compliance or malicious anomalies, while avoiding redundant manual identifications for every minor software update.

To this end, a novel risk-focused method for remotely monitoring software-driven devices subjected to legal control is proposed in this article. It is envisioned that the method will be used by market surveillance authorities and inspectors to automatically check certified devices in the field for any potential non-compliant behavior. If a device is deemed to be in violation of legal requirements after a software modification, the manufacturer would then be requested to resubmit the modified software for a complete conformity assessment procedure. The main contributions of this article are the following: The proposed method constitutes a first step towards automatic remote quality control of software-driven devices subjected to legal control. It enables automatic selection of risk scenarios based on remotely obtained behavioral data and thus also realizes functional identification of software to a certain risk background.

The remainder of the article is structured as follows: Sect. 2 provides some background on modelling and learning algorithms and presents the current state of the art in quality control for software as well as the risk assessment method currently used in Legal Metrology in the European Union. In Sect. 3, the concept of modelling certain types of measuring instruments as deterministic finite automata (DFA) is investigated. The section also outlines which preconditions need to be fulfilled to justify such an approach. Afterwards, Sect. 4 describes a novel risk-focused method of monitoring evolving software in measuring instruments based on the Active Continuous Quality Control (ACQC) approach from [18]. The implemented evaluation method is then described in more detail in Sect. 5, before it is experimentally tested and evaluated in Sect. 6 with two example test cases. Finally, Sect. 7 summarizes the main points of this article and provides suggestions regarding further work. All symbols and notations used in this article can be found in Sect. 8.

2   Background and Related Work

Certain types of algorithms can be described as finite automata. The corresponding models and how to learn the functional behavior of such algorithms, which is of particular interest during the monitoring process of potentially modified software, are described in Sect. 2.1. The methods proposed by Neubauer, Windmüller and Steffen together with Howar and Bauer [13,18], which apply active automata learning for quality control for evolving systems, are briefly described in Sects. 2.2 and 2.3 before recapitulating the previously published method of risk assessment for measuring instruments in Legal Metrology in Sect. 2.4.

2.1   Active Automata Learning

Simple state machines steered by input symbols from a finite alphabet that trigger internal state changes can be used to describe the behavior of a certain type of algorithms such as the behavior implemented in controllers for elevators, household appliances, simple digital watches etc. [16]. From a mathematical point of view, these state machines, also referred to as DFAs, are defined as a 5-tuple $(Q, \Sigma, \delta, q_0, K)$ [16] where:

1) Q is a finite nonempty set of states.
2) Σ is a set of finite input alphabets.
3) $\delta : Q \times \Sigma \rightarrow Q$ is the transition function.   (1)
4) $q_0 \in Q$ is the initial state.
5) $K \subseteq Q$ is the subset of accepting states.

To indicate whether an arbitrary input sequence has successfully been processed, DFAs may contain accepting states K which then trigger an *accept* message if such a state is reached. Otherwise, the output would be a *reject* message. It should be noted that the set K may also be empty, implying that the DFA does not contain any accepting state triggering an *accept* message. In practice, the output of an algorithm is usually more complex than such binary feedback, requiring the existence of an output symbol from a finite output alphabet Γ. Such more general state machines are referred to as Moore or Mealy automata, which can be characterized as a 6-tuple $(Q, \Sigma, \Gamma, \delta, \gamma, q_0)$ [12] where:

1) Q is a finite nonempty set of states.
2) Σ is a set of finite input alphabets.
3) Γ is a set of finite output alphabets.
4) $\delta : Q \times \Sigma \rightarrow Q$ is the transition function.   (2)
5) $\gamma : Q \times \Sigma \rightarrow \Gamma$ is the output function.
6) $q_0 \in Q$ is the initial state.

In addition to the transition function δ, describing state changes depending on the input symbol, Moore or Mealy automata also possess an output function γ that associates an output symbol with each state change. Such automata were originally conceived to represent arbitrary logic circuits and can even mimic complex IT systems at a certain abstraction level [18]. For additional details, see Sect. 2.2. To infer a DFA without having to know the exact implementation, the L^* algorithm was developed by Dana Angluin in 1987 [3]. The algorithm was later extended to the L_M^* algorithm to learn properties of the more general Moore and Mealy automata as well. Given that software changes in measuring instruments may have unknown side-effects and the instrument itself thus takes on the characteristics of a system with unknown behavior after an update, the basics of the L^* algorithm shall be briefly summarized here. See the original publication by Dana Angluin [3] for additional details of the L^* algorithm and the publication by Shahbaz and Groz [15] for an extended discussion including the L_M^* extension.

The aim of the L^* algorithm is to determine the properties of an unknown DFA by means of so-called membership and equivalence queries. To this end, the L^* learner communicates with a teacher T. The teacher abstracts the system under test (SUT), so that generic queries may be used by the learner to determine the SUT's internal DFA. If $L(A)$ is the set of strings a SUT A accepts, i.e., its language, and $Aut(A)$ is the set of all finite state machines with input alphabet Σ, then the two types of generic queries used by the learner can be defined as follows:

- Membership queries $Q_M : \Sigma^* \to \{0, 1\}$ where the learner L^* asks the teacher T to check the SUT with a given string x from the free monoid Σ^* that contains all words over Σ. If $x \in L(A)$, the response of the teacher is 1, otherwise 0.
- Equivalence queries $Q_E : Aut(\Sigma) \to \Sigma^* \cup \{true\}$ where the learner L^* asks the teacher T to perform an equivalence test between the current learned automaton representation (also referred to as hypothesis) $A' \in Aut(\Sigma)$ and the SUT A, resulting either in a counterexample $c \in \Sigma^*$ or a confirmation of the equivalence.

Internally, the L^* algorithm operates on a so-called observation table that stores results of the queries in a systematic fashion. To this end, the learner continually performs membership queries until it has constructed an initial model A'. Subsequently, it issues an equivalence query to the teacher, which either confirms correspondence between A' and A or responds with a counterexample $c \in \Sigma^*$ that fulfills either $c \in L(A) \wedge c \notin L(A')$ or $c \notin L(A) \wedge c \in L(A')$. The algorithm is completed if the obtained information is sufficient to generate a system A' with the same algorithmic behavior as the SUT A. To illustrate the outcome of the L^* algorithm, an exemplary DFA is described in Sect. 3 together with its transition function δ in tabular form in Table 1.

It should be noted, however, that the model learned by the L_M^* algorithm does not directly establish a correspondence between the known set of states Q and the derived transition function δ. Instead, most L^* and L_M^* implementations assign input symbol sequences to the states they lead to. For example, if the binary input 0 triggers a transition from the default empty state {} to a state A, that state will be represented by the input sequence 0. If another input symbol 0 then leads to a transition from state A to state B, whereas the alternate input symbol 1 leads from state A to state C, B would be represented as 00 and C as 01. From a theoretical point of view, this corresponds to building the equivalent classes of the automata congruence relation for all states. It follows that an outside examiner can match the learned transition function δ against a known reference, but it is not guaranteed that the mapping between known states in Q and learned states in Q' is correct. This observation will be revisited again and illustrated by a more detailed example in Sect. 6.

2.2 Active Continuous Quality Control (ACQC)

In [18] Windmüller, Neubauer, Steffen, Howar and Bauer presented a novel approach for ensuring compliance of an evolving complex application through active automata learning method. Their goal is to supervise and control modifications of applications throughout the entire life cycle. This is realized by establishing a consistent level for comparison via adaptive behavioral abstraction. Abstraction is achieved by means of a user-centric communication alphabet, where elements of the alphabet may correspond to entire (complex) use cases. One advantage of the method lies in its capability to identify bugs by simple examination of so-called "difference views" between consecutive models. The authors observe that software testing is in general not tailored to keep up with current, continuously evolving component-based software systems since repeatedly updating test suites for such systems is time-consuming and expensive. In [18] an incremental active automata learning method (also referred to as test-based modelling) is employed to address this issue.

To this end, daily system builds with an integrated fully automatic testing process are used in [18], where the testing process is controlled by incremental active automata learning. The proposed approach aims to address the following main problems:

- "Stable abstraction": Downward compatibility is assumed, meaning that users should not change the way they interact with the system. Nevertheless, the source code may change, but such modifications should not be apparent to the user. Therefore, the chosen abstraction mechanism is oriented on the level of use cases to facilitate comparisons between different software versions. Subsequently, the user-centric communication alphabet reflects distinct activities as part of the use cases.
- "Bridging implementation": A mechanism of the common abstraction level must ensure that any test is supported by a correct (version-dependent) implementation of an adapter for the symbols of the alphabet.
- "Maximal reuse": The central aspect of ACQC is based on the L_M^* learning algorithm for model inference. Based on selected counterexamples, the algorithm infers models from executed tests, see Sect. 2.1. One drawback of the

approach is the computationally expensive tests needed for the active learning process.

The authors observe that hypothesis models for new software releases are derived at the same level of detailedness as for the previous software release, which constitutes the main advantage of ACQC over similar approaches. Since identification of counterexamples is inherently ineffective, the derived system description will improve over time. A precise initial model is needed to enable following model-based testing. According to Windmüller, Neubauer, Steffen, Howar and Bauer, derivation of such models from source code is impractical for complex systems of a certain size. Indeed, any form of use-case-level modelling is difficult for such systems. Instead, active automata learning is used to extract models from live systems. The learned models then serve as the basis for regression tests. This approach will be reused in the method to be investigated here, see Sect. 4.

In [18] the proposed continuous quality control approach was validated by applying it to the Online Conference Service used for submitting and reviewing publications at Springer Verlag as an example with specific use cases as input symbols. Correspondingly, each input symbol represents processes like paper submission, reviewer selection or review submission. With such a high-level representation, a reasonably stable abstraction (as required above) was realized. The authors found that the chosen high-level modelling of input and output alphabets as abstraction of different use cases is well suited as a quality management facility for evolving IT systems. Not only is their method able to detect bugs, it also verifies if functional behavior of a system remains unchanged from one release to the next.

2.3 Risk-Based Testing via Active Continuous Quality Control

In [13] Neubauer, Windmüller and Steffen extended their approach to active automata learning and testing by adding a risk prioritization component. In this context, risk assessment is used to specify alphabet models which help to control the ACQC process to increase coverage of different risk scenarios. The authors explain, that today's complex IT systems usually consist of a combination of application servers with web-interfaces and third-party services. Due to the resulting heterogeneous structure, the subsequent system behavior becomes increasingly difficult to predict. During updates in particular, the combination of modified functionality and upgraded third-party components may have unintended effects. Their aim, therefore, was to continually perform automatic quality control while using risk assessment to reduce the manual labor involved in regression testing.

In this regard, platform migrations are of particular interest since user experience may drastically change, even though the underlying functionality was not intended to be modified. Of course, potential risks resulting either from a platform migration or from modified functionality cannot be automatically inferred. Therefore, the authors amended the original ACQC approach from [18] by enabling risk analysts to identify critical system aspects and prioritize them for error detection during the automatic model inference and checking steps. However, the publication [13] does not specify how risk levels are formally determined. Since risk analysts are typically not involved in software development itself, it becomes necessary to provide them with an abstraction layer that can be included in the original ACQC approach without performance loss. In [18], Neubauer, Windmüller and Steffen used the already abstract alphabet symbols which model different use cases of the SUT (see Sect. 2.2).

The authors of [13] acknowledge that there are also model-driven approaches to risk-based testing such as the one described by Lund, Solhaug and Ketil Stølen in [11]. The so-called CORAS methodology offers the possibility to perform risk assessment using well-defined software models based on UML and the Unified Process (UP). However, CORAS and similar approaches only address the modelling aspect for risk assessment and are unable to monitor and perform comparisons between subsequent models of SUTs. Neubauer, Windmüller und Steffen also observe that it is unrealistic to assume that the internal number of states of a system will not change during its entire lifecycle. Therefore, they proposed to continually repeat the learning process. This will be mirrored in the approach presented in this article, see Sect. 4.

2.4   Software Risk Assessment in Legal Metrology

One mandatory element of conformity assessment for measuring instruments consists of carrying out and evaluating a risk assessment for the instrument or type pattern to be assessed. In [5] Esche, Grasso Toro and Thiel described a method for software risk analysis particularly tailored for the software of such systems. The method is based on ISO 27005 [9] and ISO 18045 [8] and makes use of so-called assets, e.g., software, measurement data and parameters, and security properties to be matched, i.e., integrity, authenticity and availability, derived from the essential requirements from Annex I of the MID [4]. These assets include the software, parameters and data of the instrument, but also the indication of the result, accompanying inscriptions and stored data. Within the framework of this article, only the data during processing shall be considered. For such data, the MID requires integrity, authenticity and availability to detect any inadmissible influence, i.e., it must be ensured that data cannot be modified or deleted without detection and is traceable to a known source.

The next step after refining the assets for a concrete measuring instrument consists of formulating certain threats that constitute a violation of any security property for the given assets. For example, such a formal threat might read, "An attacker manages to invalidate integrity or authenticity of measurement data during processing." Given the known properties of the instrument, the assessor then identifies potential attack vectors which encompass practical technical steps to be implemented to realize the threat. Since such attacks tend to be made up of several steps which may even be shared between different threats, Esche, Grasso Toro and Thiel introduced the concept of Attack Probability Trees (AtPT) in [5]. An AtPT can be used to divide complex attacks into smaller subgoals by means of a tree representation, see Fig. 1 for an example addressing a possible

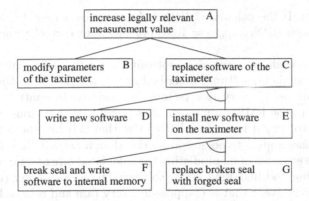

Fig. 1. Graphical representation of an attack tree that illustrates necessary steps to manipulate the calculated fare of a taximeter during processing [6]. Child nodes must be read as OR-connected, e.g., B and C, unless they are connected by an arc, which represents an AND-connection, e.g., D and E [5].

attack on the calculated fare of a taximeter. The AtPT method may be seen as an example of fault tree analysis (FTA) with an added layer that links the method to the vulnerability analysis from ISO 18045 enabling users of AtPTs to rank threats by means of a formalized and well-defined risk assessment.

In the Figure, node A, which corresponds to the threat of manipulating the measurement value, is subdivided into nodes B and C which represent the alternatives of either manipulating the measurement parameters or replacing the software of the instrument. These two child nodes may be split into further subtrees themselves. Once the tree has been established, all leaf nodes are assigned scores for required time, needed expertise, knowledge of the system, window of opportunity for an attacker and necessary equipment in accordance with the corresponding guidelines from ISO 18045 [8]. Finally, these scores are propagated up the tree as prescribed by the rules from [5] to calculate the probability of occurrence score and impact score of the original threat represented by the root node. The product of both, rounded to the next integer number, then becomes the (ideally) reproducible, numerical representation of the risk score, associated with the threat.

Apart from the concept of AtPTs or FTAs described above, there also exist other approaches to perform risk analysis, for instance the Failure Mode and Effects Analysis (FMEA) approach. The FMEA approach is often implemented within the industrial sectors where mass production of specific products is of relevance. This is due to the analysis focus of the FMEA approach which quantifies the general composite risk score with a "Risk Priority Number" (RPN) ranging from 1 to 1000. The RPN is calculated by multiplying individual risk factors such as "severity" (S), "occurence" (O) and "detectability" (D), each rated from 1 to 10 based on a given guideline, and each risk factor is assumed to be independent from each other and contributes the same importance to the calculated

RPN value [14]. If the calculated RPN value exceeds a user-defined threshold value (often taken $RPN_{threshold} = 100$), preventive or corrective actions should be taken [14].

Such an approach, however, does not suit the continuous monitoring system for modified or updated software described in this article due to the abovementioned assumptions. If every risk factor is considered to contribute the same importance as in the FMEA approach, it is possible that various combinations of each risk factor might result in a RPN value that is below the defined threshold value and may appear to possess lower risk than it actually has. For instance, considering the example of manipulating the calculated fare of a taximeter shown in Fig. 1: Writing and installing a new software on the taximeter (nodes D and E) is a very severe event that is (supposedly) very rare and relatively easy to be detected. Hence, with the FMEA approach, such a risk would be rated with a high S-score but low O- and D-scores, resulting in a relatively low RPN value. This might further cause such a high-risk event to potentially go unnoticed. On the other hand, with the AtPT approach, every potential elementary attack would be assessed and rated individually in a bottom-up fashion from the leaf nodes to the root node. Therefore, once a systematic image of all immediate or elementary attacks (leaf nodes) leading to the attack goal (root node) is identified, unwanted high-risk events could be clearly depicted and pinpointed. Consider the same example: In order to install a new software on the taximeter, the attacker needs to first "break" the electronic seal (protected logbook) of the software, overwrite the logbook to prevent backlog detection (node F) and then replace the broken seal with new forged seal (node G). Each of these events would be rated with individual occurence and impact scores, thus allowing a non-biased final risk score of the attack goal represented by the root node to be calculated.

3   Modelling Measuring Systems as Deterministic Finite Automata

In principle, finding mathematical representations, i.e., functional identifications, even for simple measuring instruments is a complex task since various physical influences need to be taken into account and must be reflected in a corresponding uncertainty budget [1]. Automatic detection of unwanted behavior of complete instruments thus quickly becomes infeasible. Nevertheless, many commonly used instruments, e.g., heat meters, typically contain internal state machines which ensure that the instrument behaves differently during installation/configuration than during permanent use. Among other qualities, heat meters have to guarantee that the installation point (either on supply side or return side of a heat generating device) can only be set during configuration and that the state cannot be reached again without physically tampering with the device. From this example, it should be clear that state machines within such instruments share many properties with DFAs and can thus be used to provide a simple example of high-level functional identification.

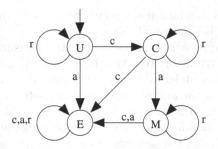

Fig. 2. DFA representing the different states of a heat meter and the state transitions. The possible heat meter states are: U for an unconfigured device, C for a configured device ready to carry out measurements, M for a measuring device and E is an error state that requires manual resetting. The input alphabet consists of the symbol c for inserting configuration dataset, a for a device activation signal and r for a request to retrieve measurement data from the device.

Table 1. Transition function δ for the heat meter example in Fig. 2. State U represents an unconfigured device, C configured yet inactive device, M a measuring device and E a device in an error state. c is the input symbol for a configuration dataset, a for an activation signal and r for a request to retrieve measurement data from the device.

		symbol		
		c	a	r
state	U	C	E	U
	C	E	M	C
	M	E	E	M
	E	E	E	E

For example, a heat meter with $Q = \{U, C, M, E\}$ would consist of the states U for an unconfigured device, C for a configured yet inactive device, M for a currently measuring device accumulating the consumed energy into a register and E for a device in a permanent error state that requires manual intervention or resetting. The input alphabet list would consist of three symbols $\Sigma = \{c, a, r\}$ where c represents the configuration of a device by feeding it a necessary datagram, a is the device activation signal and r is a request to retrieve or to read the measurement data from the device. For illustration purposes, a graphical representation of the complete DFA is given in Fig. 2. It should be noted that the depicted DFA is only a simplistic exemplary representation of the possible software states of a heat meter. In a real-world scenario, such a device would likely contain more states and more possible transitions. Also, the shown DFA only addresses the software aspects of the meter. For instance, if the permanent error state E is reached, recovery might still be possible via a manual hardware reset which is beyond the representation capabilities in Fig. 2. The corresponding transition function δ, which maps a current state to the next state given a specific input symbol, is shown in Table 1.

There exist some approaches to model both the measuring function and the DFA of measuring instruments, resulting in a so-called digital twin describing an instrument's behavior under arbitrary conditions. However, these approaches are not suitable to monitor and evaluate frequent software changes or modifications. Thus, as stated in Sect. 1, mechanisms that can automatically identify and evaluate software modifications based on risk assessment are needed.

It should be clear from the abovementioned example for heat meters, that some measuring instruments contain state machines that control the interpretation of sensor data to produce measured quantity values. Besides, if the mathematical algorithm (e.g. measurement value calculation) installed in a more complex measuring instrument is assumed to remain accurate and consistent, this state machine representation can be extended to represent the functional behavior of many other measuring instruments such as taximeters, speed measuring instruments, etc.

While certain measuring instruments include internal DFAs controlled by external input [2], such instruments usually also produce variable output data - namely the measurement result - either in digital or visual representation. Therefore, such systems fulfill the criteria of the more general Moore or Mealy automata. Nevertheless, as illustrated by the heat meter example above, many measuring instruments are already representable as simple DFAs, enabling the use of the original L^* algorithm without having to define additional output variables and resorting to the correspondingly more complex L_M^* algorithm for Moore or Mealy automata. This approach also mirrors the fact that evaluation of software security aspects in measuring instruments and evaluation of the measurement functionality are usually two separate tasks during conformity assessment of such devices. Section 4 will revisit this aspect when elaborating on a possible quality control strategy for measuring instruments in the field.

4   Risk-Based Continuous Quality Control for Measuring Systems

In [13], the authors used risk assessment to prioritize the input alphabet for the L_M^* algorithm applied to a Mealy machine to ensure quick detection of potential implementation or migration errors in evolving IT systems. In the scenario where software is updated in measuring instruments subjected to legal control, a little more flexibility might be possible given that mere bugfixes, which do not affect the functionality of the instrument, should be covered by the original conformity assessment certificate without the need to revise the certificate. To achieve this, the focus shall not be put on the choice of the input alphabet but rather on the state transitions δ discovered by executing the L^* algorithm for a new or unknown system. A graphical representation of the automatic quality control method proposed here may be found in Fig. 3.

As discussed in Sect. 2.4, performing and evaluating a software risk assessment has become an integral part of conformity assessment for most measuring instruments in the EU. During such an assessment, the risks assigned to individual threats or their subgoals can be used to derive a list of critical state transitions that the evaluator deems to be in violation or facilitate violation of the essential requirements from the MID, see top-left corner of Fig. 3. If necessary, the numerical risk scores for individual threats described in Sect. 2.4 could be used to rank new state transitions according to their risk level. In the heat meter example from Sect. 3, one such critical transition would be reverting from measurement state M back to the configuration state C, potentially leading to modified measurement parameters while a device is in use. The conformity assessment procedure could also be used to perform an initial execution of the L^* algorithm in a known environment. The initially discovered transition function δ and the known remaining elements of the DFA shall together be referred to as the model M_{old}. Continuous repeated learning of the DFA (right-hand side of Fig. 3) will produce potentially modified models M_{new} which can be compared against the previously learned and accepted model taking into account the identified list of critical state transitions. As long as no critical transition is identified, the learning loop could be repeated indefinitely to ensure that the system still operates within certified functional limits. The updated model representation also allows human evaluators to graphically identify the recent software changes and determine their potential effect. Of course, such model comparison only allows inspection of the internal DFAs of measuring instruments but neglects to address the measurement function itself. However, this approach is also used in many conformity assessment bodies in the EU where software examination (focused on the IT security of examined prototypes) and metrological examination of the measurement functionality itself (addressing measurement uncertainty, reproducibility etc.) are separate tasks that are usually conducted by separate examiners [2]. Therefore, it appears to be justified to monitor changes to the protection and security measures, e.g., the order of transitions within internal DFAs, separately from the measurement function itself.

If a critical modification is detected (if-then-statement in the lower right corner of Fig. 3), a manual intervention is needed. In order to revert the instrument to a certified state, conformity assessment for such modified instruments must be repeated. If problems are identified during re-assessment, potential corrective actions regarding improper use of non-conformant measuring instruments may be necessary. The workflow of the procedure will be illustrated by a detailed example in Sect. 6.

Figure 4 in the appendix shows a pseudocode for the general workflow of continuous quality control by learning and comparing state transitions of internal DFA models of a monitored SUT before and after modifications. From the simplified equivalence and membership queries shown in the pseudocode, it can be seen that the L^* algorithm is only dependent on the teacher and the input alphabets, thus it has an overall computational complexity of $O(\Sigma \times |Q|^2) \approx O(E)$, where E is the number of transition edges of the monitored DFA model. On

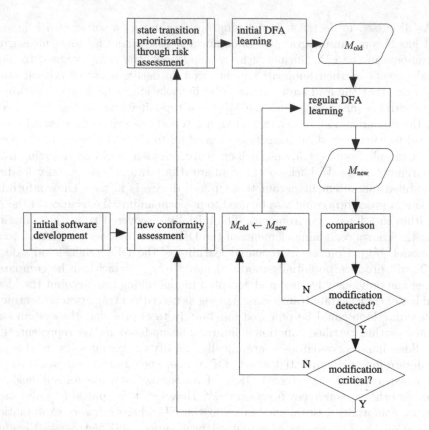

Fig. 3. Anticipated workflow of the risk-based testing approach. The initially learned model M_{old} is continually compared with newly learned models M_{new}, unless the comparison between both models identifies a critical state transition.

the other hand, the identification of critical changes in a newly learned model is naturally dependent on the implemented modification.

Depending on the complexity and size of an automaton in a SUT, learning its representation could end up being computationally expensive. Since measuring instruments usually possess rather simple DFAs and devices like taximeters usually remain inactive for longer periods on a daily basis, applying the L^* algorithm in the field to abstract such instruments still appears to be a feasible method.

It should be noted that neither L^* nor L^*_M work in actual black-box scenarios. Instead, they require the existence of a so-called teacher T during the initial learning process, which supposedly has full access to the internal automaton of the monitored SUT and can answer membership and equivalence queries accordingly, see Sect. 2.1. To this end, it is envisioned that such a teacher T could be developed by the manufacturer of the instrument and be evaluated during the initial conformity assessment. Subsequently, it could then act as a test interface for market surveillance and inspectors, enabling them to continuously monitor individual devices in the field until the need for manual intervention arises.

5 Developed Learning Algorithm Framework and Implemented Test Case Evaluation

Within the framework of this article, we developed an active state model learning algorithm based on the original L^* learning algorithm introduced by Angluin in [3] and combined this learning algorithm with some suitable test cases to feed to our self-developed test oracle. The general learning process of the implemented L^* algorithm is as described in Sect. 2.1 and the test oracle is generalized in Fig. 4 in the appendix.

In short, the evaluation of the results involves three consecutive steps: first, performing the learning process with both the membership and equivalence queries with the help of an imported teacher automaton. During the initial learning process, the teacher automaton could be provided by the manufacturer but the learned automaton could then replace this teacher automaton for the following monitoring processes. The second step consists of comparing the models and check for any difference between the original model, M_{old}, and the new model, M_{new}. Finally, the last step is either terminating the monitoring process if the detected difference is deemed critical, or updating the original model if the modified model remains conform to legal requirements.

As for the applied test cases, two main types of test cases are considered as in Fig. 5: the first type of test case focuses on the state discovery; whereas the second type of test case addresses the state transition changes between the monitoring model and the new model. Also, defining and prioritizing the critical state transitions based on the risk assessment performed as described in Sect. 4 has to be implemented in the test oracle to allow the detection of critical changes in the functional behavior of the model.

The test case regarding the state discovery is to be evaluated due to the reason that any changes in the number of states of a model should be deemed critical by default, because such changes will result in a complete change of the total use case activities and hence a functional difference in the modified model. This issue will be revisited in Sect. 6.2 again for a more detailed description. Besides, the test case regarding the state transitions is more complicated compared to the state discovery, because not all transition changes should be deemed critical to the functional behavior of a software. In order to understand the concept more clearly, the difference in the evaluation of modified critical state transitions and modified non-critical state transitions will be shown in Sect. 6.2. The evaluation of both test cases is based on an exemplary state model of a taximeter software, which is further described in Sect. 6.1.

6 Exemplary Evaluation

To illustrate the usage of the proposed risk-based ACQC workflow for measuring instruments, real-world exemplary instruments will be examined in detail as a

```
# Pseudocode of L* algorithm and risk−based testing approach

import teacher as T
import inputs as Sigma
import critical_list as crit

# Initialisation
M_old, M_new = null;

Loop:
 # Equivalence + Membership queries
 if M_new == T then
  return M_new; # equivalent model
 else
  for i = 1:Sigma:
   if Sigma(i) in T then
   # learn via input alphabets
   add (Sigma(i)) −> M_new;
  else
   # learn via counterexample
   T −> counterexample;
   add (counterexample) −> M_new;

 if M_old != null then
 # detect modified state transition
 N_mis = M_old − M_new;

 if (N_mis == 0) OR (M_old == M_new) OR (M_old == null) then
 # replace monitoring model when no modification is detected
 return M_old −> M_new;
 else if (N_mis != 0) then
 # check whether detected modifications are critical
 update crit

  if (N_mis in crit) then
   error("manual intervention.");
  else
  warning(modification learned);
  N_mis = 0;
  return M_old −> M_new;
```

Fig. 4. The pseudocode of performing L^* learning algorithm on instrument's DFA model and comparing newly learned models M_{new} with the previously learned model M_{old}. If a modification is detected, an assessment is performed to check if the legally regulated state transition is affected in M_{new} (critical) and if manual intervention for new conformity assessment is required.

```
# Pseudocode of generating test cases and prioritizing high—risk
test cases through risk assessment

import teacher as T
import critical_list as crit

compute hypothesis —> null;
risk_assessment = True; # prioritization of high—risk test cases

# generate test cases based on states
if hypothesis == null
 # test case covers all states
 test_case.state = product(T.states , 1)
else if hypothesis != T
 # test case covers remaining states excluding hypothesis
 test_case.state = product(T.states , hypothesis)
else
 test_case.state = 0;

# generate test cases based on state transitions
if hypothesis == null
 # test case covers all transitions
 test_case.transition = product(T.transitions , T.alphabets);
else if hypothesis != T
 # test case covers remaining transitions excluding hypothesis
 test_case.transition = product(T.transitions , T.alphabets ,
                                   hypothesis);
else
 test_case.transition = 0;

if risk_assessment == True
 # prioritize high—risk test cases
 sort(test_case , key = crit);
else
 # all test cases are considered even—risk
 shuffle(test_case);

append(test_case) —> hypothesis;
```

Fig. 5. The pseudocode of generating and sorting test cases based on risk assessment to be applied to the L^* learning algorithm. A hypothesis of the model is first computed which will be used for testing. The test cases are separated into two main parts: state discovery tests which detect state changes in models internal state machine; transition tests which identify changes in functional behavior of models internal state machine.

proof of concept in Sect. 6.1, followed by an investigation into different test cases, namely state and transition changes in Sect. 6.2. A discussion regarding discovery of unknown state correspondences is summarized in Sect. 6.3 and an analysis of the examples that also identifies open issues of the proposed approach in this article will be provided in Sect. 6.4.

6.1   Taximeter as a Complex DFA

A taximeter (as defined in Annex IX of the MID [4]) is a "device [that] measures duration, calculates distance on the basis of a signal delivered by the distance signal generator. Additionally, it calculates and displays the fare to be paid for a trip on the basis of the calculated distance and/or the measured duration of the trip."Therefore, the sensor is not part of this type of measuring instrument and it solely performs processing operations on the received digital distance data. This makes taximeters especially suitable as a test case for the proposed method, see Sect. 3.

Since taxis have frequently changing customers, they can usually be modelled by a DFA that mirror the process of a customer entering and leaving a vehicle as well as the starting and stopping of the measurement itself. Subsequently, said DFAs contain a state F that represents a free vehicle, whereas the DFA enters the state O to signal that the taxi is now occupied. This could either be triggered manually through a button on the device or by means of a seat contact. For the sake of a simple example, it shall be assumed that the price per travelled kilometer is fixed. It should be noted, however, that some EU member states have complex tariff structures that take current time, number of passengers etc. into account. If the occupied vehicle starts travelling, the internal DFA then enters the measuring state M. To leave this state, the customer must first pay the price, after which the driver pushes the corresponding button to exit the measurement state. In addition, most taximeters also possess an option to retrieve fiscal data, such as the overall total of calculated fares and the complete travelled distance. Both are needed to perform tax audits for taxi companies. The corresponding fiscal inspection state I can be entered if no measurement is running and it should not be possible to start a measurement from this state. Finally, some taximeters possess a functionality to perform software updates. This functionality shall be represented by a state U. A use case oriented input alphatbet would then consist of the symbols s, e, i and u. Symbol s is meant to start a measurement or transition from the free state F to the occupied state O. The symbol e correspondingly signals the intent to exit the current state and return to the default free state F. Input symbols i for fiscal inspection and u for a software update indicate the command to either perform an inspection or trigger a remote update. The corresponding graphical representation of the complete DFA may be found in Fig. 6.

The corresponding transition function δ, which maps a current state to the next state given a specific input symbol, is shown in Table 2. As indicated in Sect. 2.4, all measuring instruments must be subjected to a risk assessment as part of the necessary conformity assessment procedure before putting such instruments on the common European market. Figure 1 shows the attack probability tree as one outcome of the risk assessment procedure for a taximeter's software. When comparing the attack probability tree with the example described above, it should become clear that child node B (modification of a taximeter's parameters) cannot be linked to the transition function δ in Table 2 since there is no corresponding state that enables parameter changes. Child node C (replacing

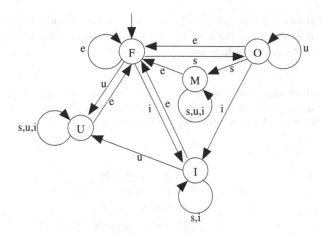

Fig. 6. DFA representing the different states of a taximeter and the state transitions. The taximeter states are F for a free vehicle with no passenger, O for an occupied vehicle, M for an ongoing measurement, I for retrieval of fiscal data and U for a software update. The input alphabet consists of the symbol s to start a measurement, e to exit a state, i to initialize fiscal review and u for a software update package. In the original model of the DFA shown here, the instrument will always return to the default state F after completing a software update in state U.

Table 2. Transition function δ for the taximeter example in Fig. 6. State F represents a free vehicle with no passenger, O an occupied vehicle and M an ongoing measurement. I represents retrieval of fiscal data and U a software update. Symbol s signifies the start of a measurement, e signifies exiting a state, i initializes a fiscal review and u corresponds to a software update package.

		symbol			
		s	e	u	i
state	F	O	F	U	I
	O	M	F	O	I
	M	M	F	M	M
	I	I	F	U	I
	U	U	F	U	U

the software of a taximeter), however, could be enabled by inadmissible transitions to and from the update state U. In fact, node E (installing new software) addresses specifically the functionality behind the update state. In this context, one should keep in mind that breaking and replacing of the seal (represented by child nodes F and G) do not necessarily have to address physical hardware seals. So-called electronic seals realized as protected logbooks are equally common in Legal Metrology [2]. Subsequently, all additional transitions to and from the update state U (represented by the detected state su in Table 3) would be classified as critical during conformity assessment since such transitions could interfere with normal processing of updates and damage the continuous audit trail of logged software modifications.

Table 3. Transition function δ obtained by L^* algorithm for the original taximeter example from Fig. 6. States are given in the representation obtained by the algorithm, e.g., sss, together with their cleartext representation, e.g., M.

		symbol			
		s	e	u	i
state	s/F	ss	s	su	si
	ss/O	sss	s	ss	si
	sss/M	sss	s	sss	sss
	si/I	si	s	su	si
	su/U	su	s	su	su

As explained in Sect. 2.2 the L^* algorithm produces a transition function δ that references the internal states of the examined DFA by their corresponding input sequences. To improve readability of the example, the first column of Table 3 contains both the cleartext representation of the states as well as their representations obtained by the learning algorithm, which correspond to the symbol sequences needed to transition to a certain state. Since s is the first symbol tested by the used algorithm, it denotes the default state F also with that symbol. Consequently, all other state representations start with that symbol, too. Section 6.3 will address how representation variations may affect the interpretation of the algorithm output and how this effect can be mitigated.

6.2   Non-critical and Critical Model Changes

In this subsection, the evaluation of different types of test cases will be discussed. In general, any modifications detected regarding the total number of states in a DFA model will be considered as critical by default; and the evaluation of transition changes in a model is separated into either critical or non-critical transitions with respect to their influence to the functionality of the model.

State Changes. With the DFA model of the taximeter described in Sect. 6.1, the proposed detection method for the state discovery test case is tested by introducing a new non-accepting, temporary state T to the DFA model, that is only reachable from the updating state U with the input symbol s (originally no transition from the state U by input symbol s), and this temporary state T is set to replicate the transitions of the original updating state, namely transitions between itself and the updating state U by the input symbols s, u and i; or between itself and the free state F by the input symbols e, see Fig. 7. This is to ensure that this modification possesses minimum influence on the functionality of the modified taximeter, hence allowing an unbiased evaluation of a detected state change in the DFA model.

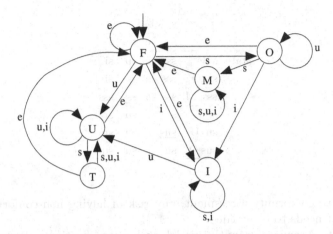

Fig. 7. DFA representing the different states of a taximeter and the state transitions after addition of a temporary state T, which causes the taximeter to have a total of six states (originally five). The temporary state is entered from state U by input symbol s (input s had originally no effect on the automaton when in state U) and has state transitions between itself and the updating state U (input symbols s, u and i), and between itself and the free state F (input symbols e).

Figure 7 depicts that the modified taximeter has a total of six states instead of the original five states. With the implemented learning algorithm in this article, the modified DFA now contains a new transition function δ as shown in Table 4. It is observed that the cleartext names of each of the original states and the representations given by the algorithm remain the same as in Table 3; and the new temporary state is represented as sus, showing the sequence of minimum input symbols to reach the temporary state from the starting state ($s/F \rightarrow su/U \rightarrow sus/T$).

By comparing Tables 3 and 4, it can be deduced that, if the simplicity of a state model is ignored, the functionality of the taximeter remains generally unchanged with the addition of the new temporary state T. Nonetheless, such a modification will be deemed critical by default regardless of the functional behavior of the model. This is due to the possibility that if the addition of new states into a model could be deemed uncritical, there exists the possibility that when sufficiently many new states, that are not contributional to the functional behavior of the model, are introduced into a state model, an "apparently equivalent state model", where the modified model appears to still consist of an equivalent transition function δ, even when the functional behavior is completely different compared with the original model. Therefore, although this may neces-

Table 4. Transition function δ obtained by application of the L^* algorithm to the taximeter example from Fig. 7 with a modification that introduced a functionally irrelevant temporary state T to the model. The corresponding modifcations in state U and the new state T, compared to the transition function depicted in Table 3, are underlined.

		symbol			
		s	e	u	i
state	s/F	ss	s	su	si
	ss/O	sss	s	ss	si
	sss/M	sss	s	sss	sss
	si/I	s	s	su	si
	su/U	sus	s	su	su
	sus/T	su	s	su	su

sitate an extra conformity assessment, any risk of having non-conform devices in the market needs to be avoided.

If any state is removed from the model, such a modification is deemed critical by default as well. A detailed evaluation will not be included in this article since the underlying reasoning remains the same as adding a new state to the model. Further discussion on the state discovery test case is covered in Sect. 6.4.

Transition Changes. To test the proposed automatic detection method for state transition changes, the DFA of the taximeter shall now be modified by adding another transition from state I for fiscal inspection to the free state F triggered by the input symbol s (originally only triggered by symbol e), see Fig. 8.

Although this transition no longer matches the original assignment linked to that input symbol, it does not constitute a critical modification from the point of view of conformity assessment. Following the learning cycle proposed in Fig. 3, the L^* algorithm is applied to the modified DFA resulting in a new version of the transition function δ, see Table 5.

As can be seen from the table, the state representation obtained by the L^* algorithm remains the same, e.g., state M is still represented by the input symbol sequence sss. The only difference between the original transition function (see Table 3) and the updated version in Table 5 may be found in the row for transitions from state si/I, where the input symbol s now triggers a return to state s/F. Since an added transition to this state was deemed uncritical during conformity assessment, monitoring of the system can be continued without the need for human intervention.

As another test case, the original taximeter DFA shall now be modified by adding a state change between update state U and measurement state M, see Fig. 9. Such a transition was deemed critical during initial assessment of the measuring instrument and should trigger an automatic response. The corresponding transition function δ learned after application of the L^* algorithm to the modified example is given in Table 6. Again, the linking between cleartext names of the states and the representations found by the algorithm appears to be unchanged.

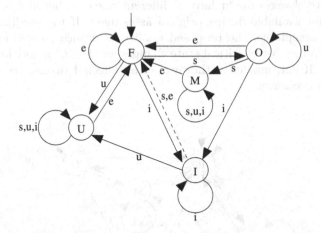

Fig. 8. DFA representing the different states of a taximeter and the state transitions after addition of an non-critical state change from fiscal inspection I to the free state F (dashed arrow). While originally only the input symbol e for exiting triggered that change, symbol s now has the same effect. In the original example, symbol s had no effect on the automaton when in state I.

Table 5. Transition function δ obtained by application of the L^* algorithm to the taximeter example from Fig. 8 with a modification that enables a second transition from I to F. The corresponding new state transition is underlined.

		symbol			
		s	e	u	i
state	s/F	ss	s	su	si
	ss/O	sss	s	ss	si
	sss/M	sss	s	sss	sss
	si/I	<u>s</u>	s	su	si
	su/U	su	s	su	su

However, as can be seen in Table 6, the transition function δ now also reflects the intended additional transition from the update state U (represented by the symbol sequence su in the table) to the measurement state M (represented by the symbol sequence sss). Since any additional transition to and from the update state was classified as critical during the original risk assessment (see Sect. 6.1), the algorithm now issues a warning that triggers a repetition of the conformity assessment procedure to check whether the modified instrument still complies with legal regulations. As part of the repeated assessment, the risk analysis would also be performed and evaluated again. During this step, the classification of critical state changes might have a different outcome because of additional information not available during original assessment. If the modified software were deemed acceptable, the proposed quality assurance algorithm would be supplied with a new list of critical state changes and the L^* algorithm would be started again. If not, manual withdrawal of all affected taximeters in the field would become necessary.

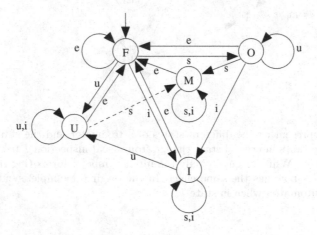

Fig. 9. DFA representing the different states of a taximeter and the state transitions after addition of a critical state change directly from the update state U to the measurement state M (dashed arrow) if the input symbol s is received. This transition is deemed critical based on the risk assessment performed on the measuring instrument and should trigger an automatic response from the monitoring process to acquire manual intervention.

6.3   Necessary Discovery of State Correspondences

As indicated in Sects. 2.2 and 6.1, the state representations by their corresponding input symbol sequences within the transition function δ obtained by the L^* algorithm depend on the order in which states are discovered. To illustrate this fact, a modified version of the original taximeter DFA shall be used, where the state transition from free state F to the fiscal inspection state I has been removed, see Fig. 10. The corresponding state transitions identified by the L^* algorithm may be found in Table 7.

Due to the different order of state discovery, the fiscal inspection state I is now no longer referenced as si but rather as ssi in the table. Since such an

Table 6. Transition function δ obtained by application of the L^* algorithm to the taximeter example from Fig. 9 with a modification that allows switching to measurement state M immediately after a software update (represented by state U).

		symbol			
		s	e	u	i
state	s/F	ss	s	su	si
	ss/O	sss	s	ss	si
	sss/M	sss	s	sss	sss
	si/I	si	s	su	si
	su/U	sss	s	su	su

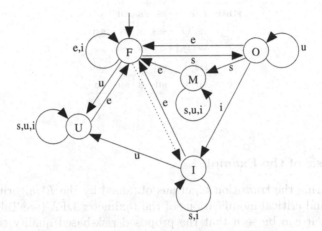

Fig. 10. DFA representing the different states of a taximeter and the state transitions after removing a state transition from free state F to the fiscal inspection state I (dotted arrow). Instead, the DFA remains in state F if an input symbol i is received in that state.

assignment of a different label could potentially affect more than one state, it becomes necessary to add a matching step to the comparison step between consecutive learned models $M_{\text{old}}, M_{\text{new}}$ included in the proposed workflow in Fig. 3. For the sake of simplicity, the matching step shall consist of checking all possible assignments between cleartext representations of DFA states and corresponding symbolic state representations from Table 2. The one assignment that minimizes the number of new or modified state transitions compared to the original DFA shall then be assumed to be correct and the identified transitions shall be evaluated against the list of critical state changes from the risk assessment. If there is more than one assignment that minimizes the number of new or modified state transitions, the state assignment is no longer unambiguous and the modification will be assumed to be critical by default. With the pseudocode shown in Fig. 11 for the matching step, this approach will only fail under two conditions:

If the overall number of discovered states does not match the original DFA (see Sect. 6.2) or if sufficiently many state changes have been implemented by the manufacturer so that the learned transition function matches the original one, even if the underlying functionality is different. Both cases will be revisited in Sect. 6.4.

Table 7. Transition function δ obtained by application of the L^* algorithm to the taximeter example from Fig. 10 after deleting one of the original state transitions from F to I.

		symbol			
		s	e	u	i
state	s/F	ss	s	su	s̲
	ss/O	sss	s	ss	s̲s̲i̲
	sss/M	sss	s	sss	sss
	ssi/I	s̲s̲i̲	s	ss	s̲s̲i̲
	su/U	su	s	su	su

6.4   Analysis of the Example

When comparing the transition functions obtained by the L^* algorithm for the non-critical and critical modifications of the taximeter DFA (see Tables 5 and 6 respectively), it can be seen that the proposed risk-based quality control approach can effectively identify and deal with both types of modifications. Manual intervention as the result of a detected assumed critical change will likely be able to assess the actual impact of the modifications and ensure compliance of all serial devices in the field.

The monitoring approach might fail, however, if several state transitions are modified or added iteratively so that they are only examined individually by the L^* algorithm. Even if the combination of modifications or additions produces effects that are in violation of legal requirements, the current implementation would not be able to detect these effects. However, this scenario is implicitly already covered by today's practice of performing periodic reverifications of measuring instruments in use. As outlined in Sect. 4, the manufacturer of the measuring instrument would need to implement a teacher T in the form of a test interface for the proposed approach to work. Of course, it cannot be guaranteed that such an interface actually interacts with the internal DFA of the measuring instrument. Instead, a dummy DFA could be implemented to hide software modifications from the automatic quality checker. During the abovementioned reverifications, however, it would be possible to also practically check whether the implemented teacher T correctly abstracts the measuring instrument's DFA for the external learner L^*, thereby mitigating such a threat. As illustrated in the example of the order of state discovery in Sect. 6.3, reproducibility of the L^* algorithm's output depends on the context-based interpretation of learned state labels.

Thereby, a brute-force matching algorithm to match all discovered states against all possible state transitions is also proposed in this article (see the pseudocode in Fig. 11) to identify the correspondences between clear text state representations and learned state identifiers. This matching algorithm will be performed after every L^* learning process but before the comparison between newly learned model M_{new} and initially learned model M_{old} (see workflow in Fig. 3). In order to avoid computation errors due to the differences in word length of discovered states, each DFA state will first be labelled as "sX", where s represents state and $X = 0, 1, 2, ...$ to make sure that similar symbol sequences in a learned model, e.g., "s", "ss" and "sss", will not be mistaken as the same state. The iterative matching process then begins with the initial state q_0 (here state F) to find the optimal match. The process continues until all discovered states are assigned their respective optimally matched known state.

```
# Pseudocode for a brute—force approach to match all DFA
    states

M_opt = null; # optimal match
N_min = 0; # mismatched transitions

    for i = 1:discovered states (M_curr):
    # replace all symbol sequences with more general state
        representation
    M_curr(s) = s(i);

    for j = 1:known states (M_know):
    # number of mismatched transitions
    N_mis = T_curr - T_know;

    if (N_mis < N_min) then
    M_opt = M_curr;
    N_min = N_mis;
```

Fig. 11. The pseudocode of brute-force matching for all DFA states. The code symbols represent M for matched model, N for number of mismatched transitions, s for state representation and T for state transitions respectively. After the initialisation, an iterative matching process starting from the first discovered state will be performed. The matching process repeats until all possible representations of state transitions are checked for each state. After the matching process, each discovered state is denoted with the known state that minimizes the overall number of mismatched transitions.

While the proposed brute-force matching algorithm is time-consuming and computationally complex, it is guaranteed to find one or more optimal matches to each state by checking all possible states against every state transitions to map them to the original model. Such an approach, however, also has several shortcomings which shall be addressed as follows:

- A brute-force matching approach might become computationally complex, if the SUT has large internal DFAs. This is due to the thorough matching process performed for every discovered and known states as shown in the pseudocode in Fig. 11. Breadth-first search algorithms, which explore a local match for each state independently, should be able to provide quicker solutions in exchange for a low chance of missing out certain transition modifications. A pseudocode for a possible implementation of a breadth-first search algorithm is given in Fig. 12. Instead of matching every state transition, the matching of a discovered state against further state transitions is halted once the current state found an apparent match. The matching process then continues with the next discovered state until all discovered states found a match.
  By comparing both matching algorithms, it quickly shows that a breadth-first search algorithm has a much lower computational complexity compared to a brute-force matching approach. While the complexity of a brute-force matching approach always remains at $O(|E_{M_{curr}}| \times |E_{M_{know}}|)$, where E represents the number of transition edges in the DFA model, this only represents the complexity in the worst case scenario of the breadth-first search algorithm, which is very unlikely to happen. Nonetheless, unlike brute-force matching where the highest possible matching accuracy for each state can be guaranteed, the implementation of a breadth-first search algorithm has a small chance of producing sub-optimal matches in certain cases. For example, both states M and U from Fig. 6 have a similar transition function, where $\delta : \{M, U\} \times \{s, u, i\} \to \{M, U\}$ and $\delta : \{M, U\} \times \{e\} \to \{F\}$. The difference between these two states lies in their respective entering state, where state M can only be entered from state O but state U can be entered from either state F or state I. When applying brute-force matching, such a difference can be detected as all state transitions will be tested. Breadth-first search however might mistakenly mix these states, thus causing a false negative modification detection when the model is compared with the initially learned model. This problem could potentially be resolved by adding extra memory to keep track of the transitions from each state, but this will not be further detailed in this article.
- As discussed in Sect. 6.2, the number of discovered states does not necessarily have to match the number of states in the original DFA, even after the application of a DFA minimization algorithm. In such a case, the currently investigated approach would always classify the modification as critical, even if a state that is not legally regulated has been removed. Although this might result in extra conformity assessment processes, such a functional identification process still causes less strain than manual identification analysis performed by conformity assessment bodies and market surveillance authorities.
- Despite high difficulty, it is theoretically possible to implement sufficiently many state/transition changes simultaneously that cannot be detected if the

learned transition function δ after the modification contains the same number of states and matching state transitions, resulting in an equivalent transition function to the original transition function.

```
# Pseudocode for a breadth—first search algorithm to find
  matching state representations

M_opt = null; # optimal match
N_min = 0; # mismatched transitions

for i = 1:discovered states (M_curr):
# replace symbol sequence with more general state
representation
M_curr(s) = s(i);

for j = 1:known states (M_know):
# number of mismatched transitions
N_mis = T_curr - T_know;

if (N_mis < N_min) then
M_opt = M_curr;
N_min = N_mis;
break;

break; # start matching the next discovered state
```

Fig. 12. The pseudocode of possible breadth-first search algorithm to detect modified state transitions. The difference between brute-force matching and breadth-first search lies in the number of matching attempts. With breadth-first search algorithm, further matching of a discovered state will be halted and the iteration restarts with another discovered state once an apparent optimal match is found. The matching process then continues until all discovered states found an apparent optimal match.

It should be noted again that the current approach only focuses on simple state transitions within DFAs while the behavior of more complex instruments than heat meters or taximeters will likely be better characterized by the more general Mealy automata, see Sect. 3. Using Mealy automata would enable checking of input and ouput behavior of such systems, thus ensuring a wider range of useful application scenarios. Investigation into an approach using the adapted L_M^* algorithm will, therefore, form the basis for further work. Similarly, machine learning algorithms such as the one described by Yan, Tang, Luo, Fu, and Zhang in [19] are already able to perform anomaly detection for complex IT systems. Due to the similarities between such systems and measuring instruments, similar approaches might also be able to model and monitor the software of measuring instruments to some extent, while potentially bridging the gap between automata models and mathematical models for measurements themselves. Once more elaborate quality control approaches for software in measuring instruments are available and have proven their reliability, it might be possible to replace mandatory periodic reverifications with risk-based reverifications based on the detected behavior of individual devices. If proven useful, such quality control approaches could be added as an acceptable solution for dealing with software modifications in the currently established technical interpretation of the MID, namely the WELMEC 7.2 Software Guide [2]. Such an acceptable solution could facilitate the uptake of the method and harmonize the approach across the EU if needed.

7 Summary

In this article, a new risk-based quality control approach for measuring instruments in legal metrology was proposed as a high-level attempt to realize functional identification for software of such systems. The approach is based on the work published in [18] and [13] that used the L^* algorithm to monitor changes in the DFAs of measuring instruments in the field. To this end, the outcome of the mandatory risk assessment procedure for regulated measuring instruments is used to identify critical state transitions to be checked if software changes occur. Based on an example for a DFA in a taximeter, the approach was evaluated regarding the detection of non-critical and critical changes, even in light of varying conditions like modified state representations. To mitigate potential effects of varying state representations, a brute-force matching algorithm was added to the proposed method that can effectively reduce the number of falsely identified transitions.

This proof of concept has shown that automatic quality control of measuring instruments is indeed possible if the SUT fulfills certain preconditions, such as a clear separation between measurement function and internal DFA. Manual intervention in case of doubt and regular reverifications are recommended to cover all eventualities. While the method requires instrument manufacturers to implement a test interface in their devices, they would benefit from the possibility of issuing bugfixes to their software without having to go through conformity assessment by default, which is the current state-of-the-art. Similarly, conformity assessment bodies would have to check said interfaces initially, but would benefit when updates are deemed to be in line with the originally certified instrument functionality, thus avoiding repetition of unnecessary software examinations. Finally, market surveillance authorities and inspectors in Legal Metrology could use the data provided by the L^* algorithm to assess modifications in devices in the field to a certain extent without the need to be on site.

It is envisioned that the approach would work in any industrial sector where software systems are used whose compliance with specific requirements must be checked by external authorities in the field. Further work will focus on validating the current approach with additional, more realistic practical test cases (also outside legal metrology) and optimizing the matching algorithm between learned and known state representations. Extending the approach from DFAs to more general Moore or Mealy automata will hopefully pave the way towards an actual functional identification mechanism for software in measuring instruments since it would also encompass the output language of devices in the field rather than simply monitor state transitions.

8 Symbols and Notations

A. Abbreviations

ACQC Active Continuous Quality Control
AtPT Attack Probability Trees
DFA Deterministic Finite Automaton
FMEA Failure Mode and Effects Analysis
FTA Fault Tree Analysis
MID Measuring Instruments Directive
RPN Risk Priority Number
SUT System Under Test

B. Symbols

A Automaton model
c Counterexample
δ State transition function
E Transition edges of a state model
γ Output function
Γ Finite output alphabets
K Accepting states
L^* Automaton-learning algorithm
$O()$ Computational complexity
q_0 Initial state
Q Nonempty-finite set of states
Q_E Equivalence queries
Q_M Membership queries
Σ Finite input alphabets
T Teacher automaton

References

1. Guide to the expression of uncertainty in measurement - part 6: Developing and using measurement models. Techreport, Joint Committee for Guides in Metrology (JCGM), BIPM, Sèvres Cedex FRANCE (2020)
2. WELMEC 7.2 Software Guide. Standard, European cooperation in legal metrology, WELMEC Secretariat, Braunschweig (2022)
3. Angluin, D.: Learning regular sets from queries and counterexamples. Inf. Comput. **75**(2), 87–106 (1987)

4. EC: Directive 2014/32/EU of the European Parliament and of the Council of 26 February 2014 on the harmonisation of the laws of the Member States relating to the making available on the market of measuring instruments. Directive, European Union, Council of the European Union; European Parliament (2014)
5. Esche, M., Grasso Toro, F., Thiel, F.: Representation of attacker motivation in software risk assessment using attack probability trees. In: Proceedings of the Federated Conference on Computer Science and Information Systems, Prague, Czech Republic, pp. 763–771 (2017). https://doi.org/10.15439/2017F112
6. Esche, M., Grasso Toro, F.: Developing defense strategies from attack probability trees in software risk assessment. In: Proceedings of the Conference on Computer Science and Information Systems, pp. 527–536 (2020)
7. Esche, M., Ho, L., Nischwitz, M., Meyer, R.: Risk-based continuous quality control for software in legal metrology. In: Proceedings of the 18th Conference on Computer Science and Intelligence Systems, pp. 445–455. FedCSIS (2023)
8. ISO/IEC: ISO/IEC 18045:2008 Common Methodology for Information Technology Security Evaluation. Standard, International Organization for Standardization, Geneva, CH, Version 3.1 Revision 4 (2008)
9. ISO/IEC: ISO/IEC 27005:2011(e) Information technology - Security techniques - Information security risk management. Standard, International Organization for Standardization, Geneva, CH (2011)
10. Jang, M.: Linux Patch Management: Keeping Linux Systems Up to Date, 1st edn. Prentice Hall, Hoboken (2006)
11. Lund, M.S., Solhaug, B., Stølen, K.: Model-Driven Risk Analysis - The CORAS Approach. Springer, Heidelberg (2011). https://doi.org/10.1007/978-3-642-12323-8
12. Mealy, G.H.: A method for synthesizing sequential circuits. Bell Syst. Tech. J. **34**(5), 1045–1079 (1955)
13. Neubauer, J., Windmüller, S., Steffen, B.: Risk-based testing via active continuous quality control. Int. J. Softw. Tools Technol. Transfer **16**, 569–591 (2014). https://doi.org/10.1007/s10009-014-0321-6
14. Shafiee, M., Enjema, E., Kolios, A.: An integrated FTA-FMEA model for risk analysis of engineering systems: a case study of subsea blowout preventers. Appl. Sci. **9**(6), 1192 (2019)
15. Shahbaz, M., Groz, R.: Inferring mealy machines. In: Cavalcanti, A., Dams, D.R. (eds.) FM 2009. LNCS, vol. 5850, pp. 207–222. Springer, Heidelberg (2009). https://doi.org/10.1007/978-3-642-05089-3_14
16. Sipser, M.: Introduction to the Theory of Computation, 2nd edn. Thomson, Boston (2006)
17. TechTopics: Functional testing - an informative guide for beginners. techreport 22, TestingXperts (2022)
18. Windmüller, S., Neubauer, J., Steffen, B., Howar, F., Bauer, O.: Active continuous quality control. In: Proceedings of the International Symposium on Component-Based Software Engineering, pp. 111–120. ACM (2013)
19. Yan, S., Tang, B., Luo, J., Fu, X., Zhang, X.: Unsupervised anomaly detection with variational auto-encoder and local outliers factor for KPIs. In: 2021 IEEE International Conference on Parallel & Distributed Processing with Applications, Big Data & Cloud Computing, Sustainable Computing & Communications, Social Computing & Networking, pp. 476–483. IEEE (2021)

A Reusability-Oriented Use-Case Model: Textual Specification Language

Bogumiła Hnatkowska(✉) ⬦ and Piotr Zabawa ⬦

Wroclaw University of Science and Technology, Wyb. Wyspianskiego 27,
50-370 Wroclaw, Poland
bogumila.hnatkowska@pwr.edu.pl
http://www.pwr.edu.pl

Abstract. Requirement specifications play an essential role in software
development processes. They can take different forms, including a use-
case model. The use-case model defines the use-cases and the relationships among them and contains definitions of the use-case specifications.
It is used to estimate software development project efforts and for planning iterations. The use-case model is subject to change as requirements
evolve or the model is refactored. Therefore, it is essential that the
use-case model is not redundant and its parts are reusable. Existing
approaches for the use-case model specification support reusability in
a limited way. This paper fills the gap. It introduces a new Use-Case
Flow Language to specify the entire use-case model conveniently yet
semi-formally. The language is defined at the abstract syntax level by
a metamodel with an informal description of the semantics of the metamodel elements. A discussion and justification of metamodel elements is
given. A concrete textual syntax of the language is also provided and
informally described. An example of a use-case model specified in the
proposed notation is presented in the paper.

Keywords: requirements specification language · use-case model ·
reusability · redundancy · abstract syntax · textual concrete syntax ·
metamodel

1 Introduction

The software requirements specification (SRS) is one of the most important artifacts documenting a software product's functional and non-functional requirements. It is always produced regardless of the development methodology used.
The SRS can take different forms, including use-case models, product backlogs
with user stories, or documents written in natural language. In the case of a use-
case model, the SRS consists of a use-case diagram presenting use-cases and
relationships among them and the associated use-case specification documents,
presenting the expected use-case behavior from the external (black-box) perspective, typically structured texts, tables, or graphical notations (e.g., activity
diagrams).

© The Author(s), under exclusive license to Springer Nature Switzerland AG 2024
A. Jarzębowicz et al. (Eds.): KKIO 2023, LNBIP 499, pp. 35–62, 2024.
https://doi.org/10.1007/978-3-031-51075-5_2

Textual specifications of the use-cases are the most widely used because they are easy to understand and quick to define, even for non-technical people. Still, on the other hand, they can be misinterpreted or incomplete [11]. Therefore, many researchers (e.g., [3,4,16]) try to define templates, a set of patterns or rules that help to keep use-case specifications complete, coherent, and consistent.

The important aspect of the use-case specification, not fully covered by existing research, is the specification reusability. There are already defined some reusability mechanisms in the UML, like «include» and «extend» dependencies and generalization. However, they are defined at the use-case level. To have an advantage of these mechanisms for use-case fragments, one should introduce new use-cases just for the reusability, which would increase the use-case number significantly, making the use-case diagram and the whole use-case model more complicated. The better solution should allow the reference to some steps, step sequences, flows, or subflows to be applied in many places without affecting the use-case structure; the change in the referenced element would influence all its instances.

The paper aims to define a language (Use-Case Flows Language, UCFL) for writing use-case model specifications, emphasizing reusability and being able for further processing, e.g. to check use-case models' completeness and correctness.

The motivation to cover the use-case model by a standardization process was and still is very strong. The reasons for standardization efforts are as follows:

- The use-case model is used for the specification of functional requirements.
- Use-case specification is the information source not only for the implementation of a software product but also for the verification of the product by functional tests; the functional tests can be implemented directly from the use-cases in parallel with the implementation.
- The use-case model is used to estimate the development efforts (see use-case points method [6]).
- Use-cases play a crucial role in iterative software development projects as the iteration plans are organized for a set of use-cases or similar constructs.
- Some commercial and research efforts tend to apply use-case models as the fundamental source of information for generating software products' source code from the model (the use-case model).

The paper is an extension of the conference paper [8] by the same authors. The extension consists of the presentations of the language genesis (Sect. 2) and the obtained results of the research (Sect. 6). Language genesis contains research objectives, which are formulated in the form independent of the solution achieved. Discussion of the research objectives is enriched with diagrams illustrating the sources of inspiration leading to the most important concepts for designing the proposed language. The results are related to the objectives, and they contain the proposed language constructs corresponding to the objectives directly.

The language specification includes the language metamodel (abstract syntax) defined in Sect. 3 and concrete textual syntax (T-UCFL) presented in

Sect. 4. The metamodel takes the form of a UML class diagram, while the concrete syntax is given in the form of context-free grammar. The notation is presented with several examples. Examples of the T-UCFL usage are contained in Sect. 5, and, finally, the content of the research presented in the paper is summarized in Sect. 7.

2   Language Genesis and Related Work

The main goal of the research is to define a new language (the UCFL) for use-case specification with additional reusability mechanisms, which do not increase the complexity of the use-case diagram itself. The existing reusability mechanisms are defined as reusable templates [15] or patterns [12,13]. None pay attention to the reusability of the step, step ranges, or global scenarios (flows).

This section presents the more detailed objectives of the research leading to reaching the above-mentioned goal. More specifically, it describes the genesis and inspiration sources for UCFL constructs, selected with the following assumptions in mind:

- UCFL can be used both at the business (summary) and the system (user) level; at the beginning, authors put stress on the latter one;
- UCFL should have both a textual and an equivalent graphical concrete syntaxes; the textual (T-UCFL) syntax will be the first;
- UCFL should follow existing good practices defined for SRS;
- UCFL should support different specification styles, e.g., action-driven and event-driven, and some advanced elements, e.g., interruptions and error handling mechanisms.

The authors looked for inspiration in the various notations used to define behavior at the business and system level, both graphical (BMPN, UML sequence, state, and activity diagrams) and textual from many existing books [3–5,16,17] and papers [6,9–15,18].

The expected benefits of the new specification language include, among others:

- processing capabilities due to its semi-formal syntax;
- use-case model complexity reduction;
- easier correctness and completeness checking of the use case specifications.

A metamodel is a typical form of abstract syntax representation, also used for use-case models [12,13]. Such a metamodel can have many different representations, both graphical and textual. The authors decided to propose their own metamodel for the use-case specification formalism to overcome existing limitations, e.g., the lack of iterations or interruptions. This metamodel is expressed in the paper in the form of the UML class diagram.

The concrete syntax of UCFL called T-UCFL takes the form of a free context grammar – such a solution was used in [9] for a similar purpose. The grammar has been developed with best practices in mind which are "built-in" in the language concrete syntax.

2.1 Use-Case Description Structure

There exist many templates for a use case textual specification. Most of them include typical sections like name, pre, and post-conditions, main, alternative, and exceptional flows, e.g., [12, 13, 15]. The template of the use-case specification structure used in the T-UCFL is given below:

```
Use-Case Model : model-name
Documentation
  Use-Case : use-case-name
    Documentation
    Preconditions
    Postconditions

    Main flow:
      1. ... -- sequence of steps

    Flow id : name
      id1. ... -- sequence of steps
```

The use case specification defines the main flow of events – sometimes called scenario [16] or basic/normal course of events [9, 17], and flows – called alternative flows [16], alternative courses (e.g. [3]), or extensions (e.g. [4]).

Instead of alternative and exceptional flows, the template simply introduces flows identified by "id" and a meaningful name. The only exception is the main flow, which does not require any specific identifier.

UCFL allows the definition of globally visible flows - specified on the use-case model level (in place of the use-case level only). A similar idea is given in [17], where the authors suggest using "several mechanisms to factor out common usage like error handling from sets of use-cases", but the idea is not formalized.

2.2 Steps Numbering

Each flow (including the main one) contains a sequence of steps defining actions to be performed. Sometimes these actions have no implicit structure, e.g. [16, 17], when the scenario is simply a sequence of sentences. In the proposed approach, the actions are classified and uniquely identified by step identifiers, which enables their reusability.

The step definition starts with the consecutive sequence number preceded by the flow identifier unless it is part of the main flow, e.g., 1. action, 2. action (for main flow), A1. action, A2. action (for flow 'A'). In case a flow starts a sub-path, the number may be followed by the identifier of the step starting the branch, e.g., A1.3 (the branch starts in step 3 of the main flow), B1.A3 (the branch starts in step 3 of the flow with identifier "A").

The step identification resembles the one proposed in [3, 15] and implemented in some tools, e.g., CaseCompleted [1] or Enterprise Architect [2]. It enables an indirect reusability mechanism, as common sub-paths of the flows are defined only once.

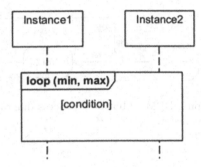

Fig. 1. A UML sequence diagram being an inspiration for the UCFL loop constructs.

2.3   Action Specification

The design of the T-UCFL supports the style of action specification based on good practices and was inspired mainly by [3,4]. The good practices applied in the T-UCFL are as follows:

- use simple grammar
- clear specification "Who has the ball"
- "checking whether" replaced by "validating"
- usage of "do steps x-y until condition" idiom

The use-case semantics, especially the control flow, must be clearly defined. This can be achieved by using specific keywords. The keywords used in the literature to represent the control flow are as follows:

- GOTO step [15] or USE-CASE CONTINUES AT step [1].
- IF-THEN-ELSE-ELSEIF-ENDIF, MEANWHILE, VALIDATES THAT, DO-UNTIL, ABORT, RESUME step, INCLUDE use-case, EXTENDED BY use-case [20].
- IF, VALIDATES, RESUME FLOW, goto, and resume statements are also defined indirectly in separate columns with appropriate names (alternative FlowId, resume FlowId) as identifiers to steps [19].
- USE-CASE CONTINUES AT, RETIRED n TIMES, ENDS IN state [14].
- COND, INVOKE, REJOIN, FINAL: state [12].

Most of them were adapted in the proposed T-UCFL, e.g., goto, validates that, includes, extends, and final.

2.4   Loops

The solution for the idiom "do steps x-y until condition" implementation in the UCFL was inspired by a UML sequence loop combined fragment (see Fig. 1).

Iterations are driven by a condition, which specifies when the iteration should stop. They also have a scope, which determines the borders of the part of something, which should be iterated. In the case of the UCFL the typical but sufficient iteration scopes are covered:

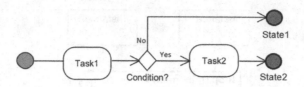

Fig. 2. Many final events on a BPMN2 business process diagram being an inspiration for the UCFL final states concept.

– a singular action
– a sequence of actions called a loop region

Additionally, one can define the minimum and maximum number of iterations.

2.5   Final States and Post-conditions

In the UCFL it is possible to define many final states, the concept of which is inspired by the BPMN2 final event concept illustrated in Fig. 2.

The UCFL-specific final action construct makes it possible to distinguish different results of a use-case flow. As a consequence, different flows may have different post-conditions associated.

Similar to [20], post-conditions can be divided into subgroups depending on the scenario and return a specific state [14]; such a construct can be used to model minimal guarantees and success guarantees.

2.6   Use-Case Relationship Constructs

Use cases can be linked with generalizations, and include or extend relationships. The links are explicitly shown on the UML use-case diagram and should be referenced in the use-case specification to keep it consistent with the diagram. The UCFL introduces special actions for the invocation of another use case, which can be unconditional (inclusion) or conditional (extension).

In the UCFL it is assumed that the parent use case in the generalization relationship must be abstract. The abstract use case does not contain any flow. This assumption does not introduce any limit to the language semantic capacity [10] – it limits the generalization construct only.

2.7   Interruptions

In the UCFL the concepts of interruptions, their handling, and resuming mechanisms are introduced. They are inspired by the UML activity diagram (see Fig. 3) and state diagram (see Fig. 4).

The interruptible regions in the UCFL are subjects of interruptions. The interruptible regions can cover:

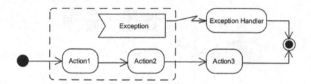

Fig. 3. A UML activity diagram being an inspiration for the UCFL interruptions concept.

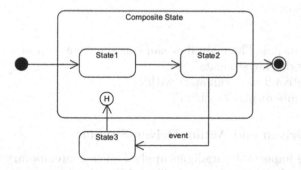

Fig. 4. A UML state machine diagram being an inspiration for the UCFL interruptions concept.

- the whole use-case model
- a specific use-case
- a sequence of actions

Thus, the interruptible regions can be nested.

To represent the "history" state in the UCFL, the context concept is introduced. It enables a description of when it is possible to resume the use-case execution after its interruption. The special "goto ctx" action serves that purpose.

2.8   Overriding Actions

Typically, the use-case behavior constitutes a complex graph of actions with many branches triggered by different conditions. It is important to be able to specify effectively how the flows are linked and under which condition the control flow may enter a particular flow in a use-case model. The problem is illustrated in Fig. 5.

Let's assume we want to model an actor's decision, e.g., "Actor wants display students" or "Actor wants display teachers". In the diagram, that is modeled in an inconvenient way for the textual notation. The first action must be defined as "Actor wants display X", and the guards e.g., "X" are students, or "X" are teachers.

To avoid these, and make the textual specification more readable, the UCFL introduces so-called overriding actions which are thought of as a shortcut for

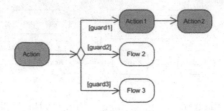

Fig. 5. A UML activity diagram being an inspiration for an approach to the UCFL flow links problem.

writing flow branches. The main flow can contain the action in the form:
3. "Actor wants display students",
and the alternative flow A can start with:
A1.3. "Actor wants display teachers".

2.9   Event-Driven and Action-Driven Support

There are some important paradigms applied when contemporary software products are designed and implemented. The UCFL supports two paradigms on the modeling level:

- event-driven modeling
- action-driven modeling

The trigger concept is present, e.g., in [4]. It is something (an event) that causes a use case to start. Triggers can be defined before any flow. This is a general mechanism as the flows may be initiated by both an actor or another flow. Alternatively, the flow's initiating action is the first action in the flow sequence.

2.10   Complexity Management with Subflows

The complexity management in the UCFL was inspired by the **ref** combined fragment of the UML sequence diagrams, a sample of which is presented in Fig. 6.

A subflow in the UCFL is a sequence of steps without an external loop (a loop leading to other step sequences). Subflows can be defined globally (at the use-case model level), and locally (at the use-case level). They belong to the main reusability mechanisms offered by the language.

3   UCFL Metamodel

This section presents the abstract syntax and semantics of the Use-Case Flow Language specification. The UCFL abstract syntax, in the form of the UML class diagram, is shown in Fig. 7. As the notation focuses on the specification of use-case behavior, the UCFL abstract syntax does not contain either actors or the relationships between them.

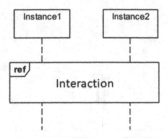

Fig. 6. References to fragments on a UML sequence diagram being an inspiration for the UCFL complexity management concept.

3.1 UCFL Containers

Container is a named element containing flows or their refinements – subflows. We have two types of containers: use-case model and use-case.

Use-Case Model. Use-case model is a container of use-cases. It can define publicly visible flows and subflows. Optionally, the use-case model can specify so-called use-case model interruptible regions or flow-interruptible regions (see Sect. 3.7) and be documented by a string.

Use-Case. Use-case is a basic modeling element that represents interactions between the system and its actors via flows and subflows. It may have optional documentation describing the use-case goal. The use-case may also specify use-case interruptible regions (see Sect. 3.7).

Pre and Postconditions: A use-case may require some preconditions to be met in order to enable the use-case behavior. These preconditions (if any) are sentences in natural language. The use-case behavior can change the state of the system. The state changes are represented by postconditions. Each postcondition is a sentence in natural language with a state name, e.g., success, partial success, failure, or other, defined by a modeler.

Generalization: Use-cases can be related to each other with generalization relationships. A use-case can be the parent of many use-cases (children). Only leaves of the inheritance tree can have flows defined. A justification for this decision is given later in this section.

3.2 UCFL Container Elements

Flow. Flow is a key element used to structure the use-case behavior. It is a sequence of steps referring to actions performed either by an actor or by the system. A step has a sequence number and a step identifier constructed from the flow identifier.

From the perspective of a graphical language representation, a flow is a path (possibly looped) in the graph without any branches. Flows can be assembled

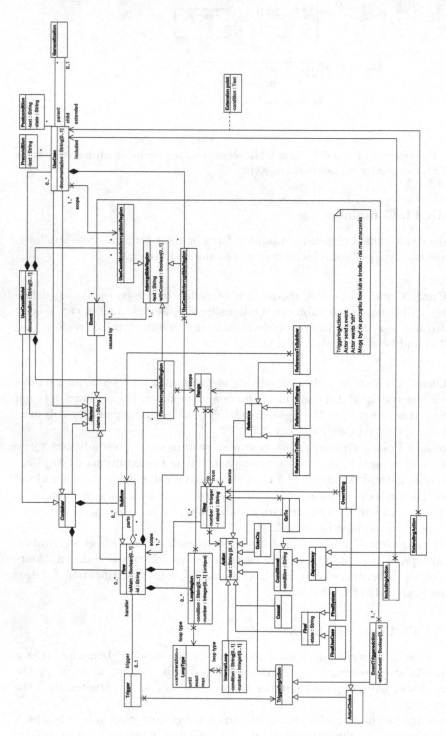

Fig. 7. UCFL abstract syntax

into a graph using specific actions, e.g., conditional. The first action in the flow can connect it to another flow (as a branch of another flow) - see Fig. 8.

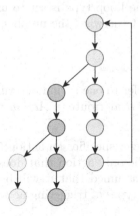

Fig. 8. Flow visualization – different flows are represented by different colors

The flow declaration introduces a flow identifier and a name (both of which must be unique within the context of the flow owner) and, optionally, a trigger. A trigger specifies an action (called a triggering action) that enables the flow. If the flow has a trigger, the flow is called a handler. If the owner of the flow is a use-case then the flow can be marked as a main flow (a use-case must define exactly one main flow; other flows are alternatives).

A flow can additionally define flow interruptible regions (see Sect. 3.7) and loop regions (see Sect. 3.5).

A flow can be constructed from subflows.

Subflow. Subflow is a specialized flow with the restriction that its steps must refer to actions that form a sequence that is casual, finals, and internal loops actions (see Sect. 3.6). The subflow is a primary reusable element. It can be shared by several flows; however, a subflow cannot contain interruptible regions or loop regions.

3.3 Range

Range is a sequence of steps (from–to) included in one flow. Ranges define the scope of flow interruptible regions (see Sect. 3.7) or loop regions (see Sect. 3.5).

3.4 Loop Type

Loop type is an enumeration of literals defining different types of loops: `until` (do something until condition), `exact` (do something the exact number of times), `max` (do something the maximum number of times). The type is specified when defining a loop region or an internal loop action.

3.5 Loop Region

Loop region is the specification of a range that can be repeated in the manner defined by a Loop type. If the Loop type is set to until, the condition for the loop region must be defined. Otherwise, the number attribute must be set.

3.6 Actions

Each step of the flow must refer to one action describing the actor-system interaction in an informal way (*text* attribute in *Action* metaclass).

Triggering Actions. A trigger specifies an action (so-called triggering action) that enables the flow. It is the only action that does not need to be referenced by a flow step because it is assumed that it will be performed by an actor to start the flow. There are two types of triggering actions: actor choice action and event-triggered action.

Actor Choice Action: A flow can be started at the request of the actor, represented by the Actor's choice triggering action.

Event-Triggered Action: A flow can be started by an actor sending an event to the system, which is modeled by an event-triggered action.

The event-triggered action must refer to an event and optionally can contain a request to store the context before the event is handled (attribute *withCtx*). The event is understood as something that happens at a specific time that requires the system reaction. The event has a name that serves as an event identifier. The context defines the name of the running flow or subflow within the region scope (if any) and its running step, which allows the behavior to be resumed later.

Casual Action. Casual action is the most general. It is used to model anything the actor or system must do, that cannot be expressed by other actions.

Finals. A modeler can define a final action to express that the system has completed its operation (Final system action) or that a use-case has completed its operation in a particular state (Final use-case action). Such an action should be the last one in the flow (or subflow in the case of the final system action).

Conditional. Conditional action represents a decision made by the system under specific conditions. Such an action may check whether another use-case has ended in a particular state. It is usually the first action of the alternative flows.

Internal Loop. Internal loop represents a case where a particular action is to be repeated in the manner defined by the loop type (see Sect. 3.4 for details).

GoTos

GoTo: Goto action is used to define unconditional loops. You can jump to a particular step in the same flow or any flow in the same use-case provided that the referenced step exists.

GoTo Ctx: The special version of goto action - Goto ctx - allows you to return to the previously saved context (the interrupted action is executed again).

Overriding. Overriding is a specific action used as a branching mechanism in the flow definition. This action points to the step in the base flow that is being overridden. The action in the source step must be of the same type as the parent of the overriding action (Actor choice or Conditional).

References. References represent the reusable elements of the UCFL. Depending on the scope of reusability, three types of reference are distinguished: reference to step, reference to subflow, and reference to range.

Reference to Step: Reference to step is the simplest reference action, where the scope of reusability is limited to a single action defined in the step to which the reference action refers. You can imagine that the reused action is copied in place of the reference to the step action.

Reference to Subflow: Reference to subflow is the reference action in which the scope of reusability is a particular subflow. When the subflow activity is finished, the control flow is passed back to the original flow.

Reference to Range: Reference to the range is the reference action in which the scope of reusability is limited to a specific range.

Dependencies. *Including*: A use-case can include the behavior of another use-case. The semantics of this action is similar to the «includes» relationship in the UML [5] where the including use-case is the owner of the flow with the including action, and the included use-case is the one indicated by the including action.

Extending: The flow of a use-case can contain an extending action. The semantics of this action is like the «extends» relationship in the UML [5] where the extended use-case is the flow owner with the extending action, and the extending use-case is that indicated by the extending action. The extension point describes a condition that must be satisfied for the extension to take place.

3.7   Interruptible Regions

The UCFL allows the definition of interruption (exception) handling mechanisms using so-called interruptible regions. Such a region points to its scope. The scope of the region can be either a set of use-cases (use-case model interruptible region), a set of flows defined within a use-case model, or a use-case (use-case interruptible region), a range (flow interruptible region). The scope can be interrupted by any event, that caused the interruption.

Use-Case Model Interruptible Region. Use-case model Interruptible Region enables specification of the interruption mechanisms at the use-case model. The interruption scope can refer to any flow or a use-case defined in this container.

Use-Case Interruptible Region. Use-case Interruptible Region enables specification of the interruption mechanisms at the use-case level. The interruption scope can refer to any flow defined in this container.

Flow Interruptible Region. Flow Interruptible Region enables specification of the interruption mechanisms at the flow level. The interruption scope can refer to a range (step from, step to) defined in the flow context.

3.8 Use-Case Generalization Relationship

Use cases are classifiers and can inherit one from another. An example of such inheritance is shown in Fig. 9. Assuming that the use-case specification is given in natural language, the question arises of how the use-case generalization influences their specification, which can "include possible variations of its basic behavior, including exceptional behavior and error handling" [5].

Generally, a behavior is a specification of events that may occur during the use-case lifetime. The specification must contain at least one event – the event of its invocation [5]. The behavior is invoked when an instance of the owning classifier (i.e., use-case) is created.

In the case of use-case inheritance, a child's specification of events (including the triggering one) is inherited from the parent use-case, which makes the whole specification ambiguous. Therefore, to avoid possible problems and misinterpretations, we assume that any parent use-case must serve only as a root of a use-case hierarchy. Use-case triggers for the hierarchy leaves should determine which child to run.

4 T-UCFL Informal Description

This section demonstrates the use of the T-UCFL concrete syntax [7] with several examples. The language grammar has been designed to keep the language flexible and concise. However, as the specification is intended to be processed by computers, the grammar may impose some constraints on the use of the language, such as the need to enclose elements in quotes or the use of certain keywords.

4.1 T-UCFL Containers

The container – as an abstract class – has no textual representation.

Use-Case Model. A use-case model is a container and a namespace for all other elements. Its declaration defines the model's name (e.g., Buying) and optional documentation. Its definition contains shareable elements with global visibility (flows and subflows), an optional declaration of interruptible regions, and a list of use-cases. The concrete syntax assumes that the documentation is textual; however, for readability purposes, the authors decided to use a graphical version in the example presented below (see Fig. 9).

```
Use-Case Model: Buying
Documentation:
```

```
Use-Case Model: Buying
Documentation:
```

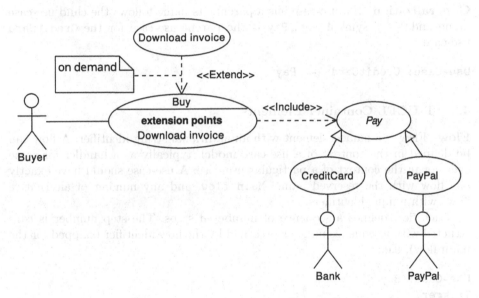

Fig. 9. Buying use-case model documentation in the form of a use-case diagram

Use-Case. Use-case specification consists of a use-case declaration followed by the use-case definition. The use-case declaration defines a unique use-case name within the use-case model (e.g., CreditCard) and, optionally, use-case documentation.

```
Use-Case: CreditCard
Documentation: "Use-case enables payment with a credit card."
```

Pre and Postconditions. A use-case declaration can also contain pre- or post-conditions placed after documentation (if any). The precondition section has one or more statements expressing conditions, for example

```
Preconditions:
- "Actor is logged in the system."
```

Quotation marks are required by formal grammar and can be skipped if the use-case specification is not going to be automatically translated.

Each post-condition section, if any, should define a name of a final system state name (e.g., success, partial-success, error) followed by one or more conditional statements, e.g.,

```
Postcondition(success):
- "An order is stored by the system."
```

Generalization. If a use-case has a parent, its name follows the child use-case name and "-->" symbol, e.g., `Pay` is the parent use-case for the `CreditCard` use-case:

```
Use-Case: CreditCard --> Pay
```

4.2   T-UCFL Container Elements

Flow. Flow is a named element with an additional string identifier. A flow can be defined in the context of a use-case model, typically as a handler for some event or in the context of a particular use-case. A use-case should have exactly one flow with the reserved name: `Main flow`, and any number of alternative flows with unique identifiers.

Each flow defines a sequence of numbered steps. The step number is constructed with a sequence number preceded by the flow identifier (skipped for the main flow), e.g.:

```
Use-Case: Buy
Trigger: ...
Main flow:
  1. ...
  2. ...
Flow B: The_order_data_invalid
  B1. ...
Flow C: Unsuccessful_payment
  C1. ...
```

The example shown above presents the Buy use-case with the main flow and two alternative flows B and C (B is the identifier, `The_order_data_invalid` – is the flow name). The main flow of the use-case has a triggering action defined.

Subflow. A subflow is an element of reuse. It can be visible globally (subflows defined at the use-case model level) or locally (subflows defined at the use-case level). They serve to split long flow definitions into manageable fragments. Only casual, final, and internal loop actions are allowed in the subflow definition.

A subflow example is given below:

```
Subflow P: Car_info
  P1. ...
  P2. ...
```

4.3 Range

Range defines a subsequence in a flow, identified by two steps identifiers, e.g., 2.-3. consists of 2 steps (2 and 3 in the Main flow), A.5.-A.7. consists of 3 steps in the flow A.

4.4 Loop Type

Loop type is a keyword (one of until, exact, max) used together with a loop region or internal loop action to specify the loop type – see Sect. 5 for examples.

4.5 Loop Region

The loop region works in a similar way to an interruptible flow region. It specifies a range of steps to be repeated as specified by the associated loop type. The loop region is placed after all the steps of the flow, e.g.,

```
Main flow:
  1. ...
  2. ...
Steps 1-2 can be repeated exactly 3 times
Steps 1-2 can be repeated until "condition."
```

4.6 Actions

Triggering Actions. A triggering action is typically used to specify how an actor starts a particular flow. In this case, it is specified before the flow, after the Trigger keyword. Examples of triggering actions include Actor choice action or Event-triggered action. However, the triggering actions can also be referenced by flow steps.

Actor Choice Action: A flow can be started by an actor (their decision). Such action must start with Actor wants and be followed with "decision" written in quotation marks, e.g.,

```
Use-Case: CreditCard --> Pay
Trigger: Actor wants "to pay with a credit card"
Main flow: ...
```

Event-Triggered Action. A flow can also be started by an event sent asynchronously by an actor. Such an action must start with `Actor sends` and be followed with the event name and one of `event` or `event with ctx`, e.g.,

```
Actor sends cancelling_service event
Actor sends cancelling_service event with ctx
```

The latter action contains the request to store the context before the event is handled.

Casual Action. Casual action is the most general. It is a free text without keywords present in other types of actions like `verifies`, `includes`, `ends with` or `goto` (e.g., `"System asks about the order data"`), representing something that the actor or the system must do. The grammar requires this action to be enclosed in quotation marks.

Finals. The modeler can define a final action expressing that the system finishes operation (`The system ends`) or a use-case finishes in a specific state (e.g., failure) with the phrase: `The use-case ends with failure`. Such an action should be the last one in the flow. The first one means that the system stops running.

Conditional. The conditional action represents a decision made by the system. It must contain the phrase `System verifies` or `System verifies that`, followed by a phrase containing a condition, e.g.,

```
System verifies that "the order data are valid".
```

Such an action may check whether another use-case ended in a specific state, e.g. (`System verifies that Pay use-case ended with failure`).

Internal Loop. One can define that a given action should be repeated a specific number of times specifying its loop type, e.g.,

```
- "Actor selects products" max 3 times.
- "Actor selects products" until "he is satisfied".
```

GoTos. *GoTo*: GoTo action is used to define unconditional loops. We can jump to a particular step in any flow defined in the specific context (a use-case model or a use-case) provided that the referenced step exists, e.g., `Goto 2.` (a jump to the 2nd step in the `Main flow`), `Goto A3.` (a jump to the 3rd step of flow `A`).

GoTo Ctx: GoTo ctx is a special version of the goto action that passes the control flow to the previously saved context (if any). If no context is stored, the semantic is undefined. The interrupted action defined by the context is executed again.

Overriding. Overriding actions are used to link flows in a graph. They point to the action in another flow and should be of the same type as the overridden action. Typically, they start alternative flows in a use-case. An example of an overriding action when a decision is made by the system might look like this:

```
B1.3. System verifies that "the order data are invalid"
```

The 3rd step in the main flow will be overridden in the B flow with the action given above.

References. A reference is a basic reusability mechanism. One can reuse another step, step range, or subflow behavior. Examples of such actions are given below:

- A1.2. (a step reference; in the 1st step of flow A, the 2nd step of the main flow is reused)
- A2.B3. (a step reference; in the 2nd step of flow A, the 3rd step of flow B is reused)
- B3.A1.-A2. (a range reference; in the 3rd step of the flow B, the range of two steps 1–2 from the flow A is reused)

Technically, the reference to a singular step or step range can be thought of as a shortcut for a preprocessing mechanism that copies the referenced elements to the places where they are used and renumbers the steps respectively. Let us assume that flow A contains the steps:

```
A3. Action 1
A4. Action 2
```

and that flow B contains the steps:

```
B1. Action 3
B2. A3.-A4.
B3. Action 4
```

The result of such preprocessing can look like this:

```
B1. Action 3
B2.a. Action 1
B2.b. Action 2
B3. Action 4
```

Subflows must be directly referenced (keyword `subflow` followed by the subflow name) in the appropriate actions, e.g.

```
A2.subflow Car_Info
```

Dependencies. *Including*: One use-case can include or extend another use-case behavior. This is modeled with dependency actions: including or extending. An example of the including action is given below:

```
System includes Pay use-case.
```

When the included use-case reaches the final action, the control returns to the including use-case.

Extending: Two use-cases can also be linked with an extension relationship. The flow of the extended-use case should contain the extension point definition, e.g.,

```
Extension point: "Actor requires the invoice downloading."
```

The flow is extended with `Download_invoice` use-case.

The extension point specifies a condition under which the flow is extended with another behavior (here: "Actor requires the invoice downloading"). The control returns to the extended use-case when the extending use-case reaches the use-case final action.

4.7 Interruptible Regions

An interruptible region defines a scope for which the normal operation of the system can be interrupted by a specific event (its name is given) coming from an actor.

Use-Case Model Interruptible Region. Use-case model interruptible region is the one with the widest scope. If it is present, it is placed at the beginning of the use-case model definition, e.g., where any use case can be interrupted by the `close_system` event.

```
Use-Case Model: Document_Editor
Any use-case can be interrupted by close_system event
```

Use-Case Interruptible Region. The scope of a use-case interruptible region is limited to a specific use-case. If it is present, it is placed at the beginning of the use-case definition, e.g.,

```
Use-Case Model: Buy
Any flow can be interrupted by close_system event
```

Flow Interruptible Region. The scope of a flow interruptible region is limited to a range within a specific flow. If it is present, it is placed after all flow actions, e.g.,

```
1. ...
10. The use-case ends with success
Steps 1.-3. can be interrupted by
  cancelling_service event with ctx
```

The flow interruptible region narrows the scope of the event handling mechanism, e.g., the interruption will be only handled within between steps 1–3 (inclusively).

5 Example Specification

A small example of a use-case model is contained in this section. The model is shown in Fig. 9 and it was specially designed to show most of the constructs, which are introduced informally in Sect. 4.

The model-related part of the T-UCFL specification is the first one:

```
Use-Case Model: Buying
Trigger: Actor sends cancelling_service event
Flow A: Cancelling_service_event_handler
  A1. "System asks for cancellation confirmation"
  A2. Actor wants "to cancel the operation"
  A3. The use-case ends with failure

Flow B: Cancellation_denied
  B1.A2. Actor wants "to deny cancellation"
  B2. Goto ctx
```

The above model specification consists of the use-case model called Buying; global flow A named Cancelling_service_event_handler; the global flow B named Cancellation_denied. The Cancelling_service_event_handler is shared among all use-cases and can be triggered by the cancelinig_service event generated by an actor. In turn, the Cancellation_denied is a branch of the A flow (see a reference step B1.A2.). The Goto ctx action (if performed) is intended to pass the control flow to the previously remembered context.

The subsequent use-case specifications constitute the remaining parts of the T-UCFL specification.

```
Use-Case: Buy
Postcondition (success):
- "An order is stored by the system"
- "An invoice is generated, assigned
  to the order, and stored by the system"

Trigger: Actor wants "to buy an item"
Main flow:
  1. ...
  2. "System asks about the order data (including payment method)"
```

```
    3. "Actor delivers the order data"
    4. System verifies that "the order data are valid"
    5. System includes Pay use-case
    6. System verifies that "the Pay use-case ended with success"
    7. "System stores an order, generates an invoice,
       and sends it by e-mail"
    8. "System informs about order completion and enables an option
       to download the invoice"
    9. Extension point: "Actor requires invoice downloading"
The flow is extended with Download_invoice use-case
    10. The use-case ends with success

Steps 1.-3. can be interrupted
    by cancelling_service event with ctx
```

Several conditional actions (e.g., 4, 6) form the main flow. An including action (Pay use-case is included) can be found as the 5th step of the main flow. An extending action with a condition defined is contained in the 9th step. There is also a flow interruptible region, which consists of steps range 1.-3..

After the main flow two alternative flows (B and C) are specified:

```
Flow B: The_order_data_invalid
    B1.4. System verifies that "the order data are invalid"
    B2. "System informs about invalid data"
    B3. Goto 2.

Flow C: Unsuccessful_payment
    C1.6. System verifies that "the payment ended with failure"
    C2. "System informs about the lack of payment"
    C3. Goto 2.
```

The first step of both alternative flows refers to the step with conditional action in the main flow. The condition associated with the mentioned first step complements the condition from the conditional action in the main flow just to form the main flow alternatives correctly.

The specification continues with the Download_invoice use-case specification:

```
Use-Case: Downolad_invoice
Postcondition (success):
- "An invoice is downloaded to the Buyer's computer"

Main flow:
    1. "System presents the invoice details and asks
       for confirmation of the invoice download"
    2. Actor wants "to download the invoice"
    3. "System sends the last buyer invoice to the buyer's computer"
```

```
  4. The use-case ends with success
Steps 1.-3. can be interrupted
  by cancelling_service event with ctx

Flow B : Downloading_not_confirmed
  B1.2. Actor wants "to skip downloading"
  B2. The use-case ends with partial success
```

The use-case has only one alternative flow B, which – in contrast to the Buy use-case, is started by the actor's choice action.

There are three interrelated use-cases in the Buying use-case model. The Pay abstract use-case does not contain a flow and has the following form:

```
Use-Case: Pay
Documentation: "Abstract use-case. A root hierarchy for different
  payment methods"
Postcondition (succes):
- "payment succesfull"
Postcondition (failure):
- "payment unsuccesfull"
```

The above Pay abstract use-case is the parent for two concrete use-cases (CreditCard, PayPal), which are also contained in the example T-UCFL specification. Below, the specification of the CreditCard use case is presented.

```
Use-Case: CreditCard --> Payment
Documentation: "Use-case enables payment with a credit card"
Trigger: Actor wants "to pay with a credit card"
Main flow:
  1. "System asks for credit card details"
  2. "Actor delivers credit card details"
  3. "System sends a request to a bank for payment and waits
     for bank response"
  4. System verifies that "the payment was successful"
  5. The use-case ends with success
Steps 1.-3. can be interrupted by cancelling_service event

Flow B: Payment_unsuccessfull
  B1.4. System verifies that "the payment was unsuccessful"
  B2. The use-case ends with failure
```

The repository created by the authors at [7] contains more examples with the T-UCF constructs not presented in the example.

6   Results

The research objectives are presented in Sect. 2. This section summarizes the results of the research presented in the form of the T-UCFL constructs. Each such construct is related to the objectives directly.

6.1 Steps Numbering

The steps numbering concept applied in the T-UCFL makes it possible to reuse subpaths as well as it allows to nest the alternative flows without limits. An example T-UCFL construct with steps numbering is presented below.

```
Main flow:
  1. Action 1
  2. Action 2
  3. Action 3

Flow A: alternative_1
  A1.2. Action 5
  A2. Action 6

Flow B: alternative_A1
  B1.A2. Action 7
  B2. Action 8
```

6.2 Use-Case Relationships

A use-case specification may contain any use-case relationship expressed on the use-case diagram in the following forms:

– inclusion

```
  6. System includes Pay use-case.
```

– extension

```
  6. Extension point:
  "Actor requires the invoice downloading."
  The flow is extended with Download_invoice use-case.
```

– generalization

```
  Use-case: Credit card --> Pay
```

6.3 Iteration Scope

Iteration scope in the T-UCFL may be one of the following:

– a singular action
  - "Actor selects products" max 3 times.
  - "Actor selects products" until "he is satisfied".
– a loop region

```
  Main flow:
  1. ...
  2. ...
  Steps 1.-2. can be repeated exactly 3 times.
  Steps 1.-2. can be repeated until "condition".
  Steps 1.-2. can be repeated max 3 times.
```

6.4   Subflow

The Subflow concept introduced in the T-UCFL can be expressed in the form of the following constructs.

```
Subflow P: Test
  P1. ...
  P2. ...
Use-case : Demo
Main flow:
  1. Subflow Test
```

6.5   Interruptible Regions

The concept of interruptible regions is implemented in the T-UCFL at the three levels:

- the use-case model level:

  ```
  Use-Case Model: Document_Editor
  Any use-case can be interrupted by close_system event
  ```

- the use-case level

  ```
  Use-Case Model: Buy
  Any flow can be interrupted by close_system event
  ```

- the interruptible region level

  ```
  1. ...
  10. The use-case ends with success

  Steps 1.-3. can be interrupted
      by cancelling_service event with ctx
  ```

6.6   Overriding Action

The realization of the overriding action concept is illustrated in the form of the following T-UCFL expressions.

```
Flow A: Cancelling_service_event_handler
  A1. "System asks for cancellation confirmation"
  A2. Actor wants "to cancel the operation"
  A3. The use-case ends with failure

Flow B: Cancellation_denied
  B1.A2. Actor wants "to deny cancellation"
  B2. ...
```

6.7   Triggers

Triggers concept is illustrated in the form of the following T-UCFL expressions.

```
Trigger: Actor sends cancelling_service event
Flow A: Cancelling_service_event_handler
  A1. "System asks for cancellation confirmation"
  ...
```

6.8   Basic Reusability Mechanisms

The following T-UCFL constructs illustrate the references, which are in turn one basic reusability mechanism.

– a step reference

```
A1.2.
A2.B3.
```

– a range reference

```
B3.A1.-A2.
```

– a subflow reference

```
C4. subflow Test
```

7   Summary

The paper introduces a new concept of a reusability-oriented approach to use-case model specification. The need to put emphasis just to the use-case modeling reusability was recognized during the commercial activities of the authors. As the result of the in-depth research, a new use-case model specification language named Use-Case Flow Language (UCFL) is proposed in the paper. The UCFL consists of the metamodel and a Textual Use-Case Flow Language (T-UCFL), which is a textual concrete syntax of the UCFL. The T-UCFL is introduced as a medium for use-case behavior specification.

The syntax of the T-UCFL is stable, which results from the multiplicity of advanced experiments conducted. The experiments were focused on modeling a lot of non-trivial behaviors of several specially invented software systems. The UCFL metamodel was inferred just from these experiments.

The main purpose of designing the concepts introduced in the paper is extensive reusability support and avoidance of redundancy in use-case flows. The initial fragments of the flows are reused by definition – they are shared with alternative flows. There is a possibility to form references to a singular step, steps range, or a subflow. As the result of the reusability and elimination of redundancy, the change introduction is much simpler than the one known from other approaches to use-case modeling. A change made in one place is reflected in many places referring to the changed element. Inclusion, extension, and generalization as the inter-use-case relationships are supported as well.

The use-case specification expressed in the UCFL mimics the specification written in a natural language. This special nature of the UCFL is a result of some general UCFL features – it is internally consistent, concise, and semi-formal.

The paper introduces the UCFL abstract syntax and a textual concrete syntax. Nevertheless, many other concrete syntaxes may be introduced, including graphical ones.

The UCFL is planned to be further developed as it seems to be very promising. The authors intend to extend the notation introduced in the paper with tool support. The already mentioned graphical concrete syntax is the subject of research together with bidirectional transformation between concrete syntaxes. The usability of the UCFL needs to be validated by external users, first at universities and then in the IT industry.

References

1. CaseCompete. Technical report. https://casecomplete.com
2. Enterprise architect. Technical report. https://www.sparxsystems.com
3. Adolph, S., Bramble, P., Pols, A.: Patterns for Effective UseCases. Addison-Wesley Professional (2003)
4. Cockburn, A.: Writing Effective Use-Cases. Addison-Wesley (2000)
5. Cook, S., et al.: Unified modeling language (UML) version 2.5.1. Standard, Object Management Group (OMG), December 2017. https://www.omg.org/spec/UML/2.5.1
6. Diev, S.: Use cases modelling and software estimation: applying use case points. ACM SIGSOFT Softw. Eng. Not. **31**(6), 1–4 (2006). https://doi.org/10.1145/1218776.1218780
7. Hnatkowska, B., Zabawa, P.: Use-case flow (UCF) case-studies. Repository (2023). https://github.com/bhnatkowska/UCF
8. Hnatkowska, B., Zabawa, P.: A reusability-oriented use-case model specification language. In: Conference on Computer Science and Information Systems (2023). https://api.semanticscholar.org/CorpusID:264118179
9. Iqbal, S., Al-Azzoni, I., Allen, G., Khan, H.U.: Extending UML use case diagrams to represent non-interactive functional requirements. e-Informatica Softw. Eng. J. **14**(1), 97–115 (2020). https://doi.org/10.37190/e-Inf200104
10. Krótkiewicz, M., Jodłowiec, M.: Modeling autoreferential relationships in association-oriented database metamodel. In: Świątek, J., Borzemski, L., Wilimowska, Z. (eds.) ISAT 2017. AISC, vol. 656, pp. 49–62. Springer, Cham (2018). https://doi.org/10.1007/978-3-319-67229-8_5
11. Liu, S., et al.: Automatic early defects detection use case documents. In: Proceedings 29th ACM/IEEE International Conference on Automated Software Engineering, pp. 785–790 (2014)
12. Śmiałek, M., Ambroziewicz, A., Parol, R.: Pattern library for use-case-based application logic reuse. In: Lupeikiene, A., Vasilecas, O., Dzemyda, G. (eds.) DB&IS 2018. CCIS, vol. 838, pp. 90–105. Springer, Cham (2018). https://doi.org/10.1007/978-3-319-97571-9_9

13. Śmiałek, M., Bojarski, J., Nowakowski, W., Ambroziewicz, A., Straszak, T.: Complementary use case scenario representations based on domain vocabularies. In: Engels, G., Opdyke, B., Schmidt, D.C., Weil, F. (eds.) MODELS 2007. LNCS, vol. 4735, pp. 544–558. Springer, Heidelberg (2007). https://doi.org/10.1007/978-3-540-75209-7_37

14. Mustafiz, S., Kienzle, J., Vangheluwe, H.: Model transformation of dependability-focused requirements models. In: Proceedings ICSE Workshop on Modeling in Software Engineering, pp. 50–55 (2009)

15. Ochodek, M., Koronowski, K., Matysiak, A., Miklosik, P., Kopczyńska, S.: Sketching use-case scenarios based on use-case goals and patterns. In: Madeyski, L., Śmiałek, M., Hnatkowska, B., Huzar, Z. (eds.) Software Engineering: Challenges and Solutions. AISC, vol. 504, pp. 17–30. Springer, Cham (2017). https://doi.org/10.1007/978-3-319-43606-7_2

16. Overgaard, G., Palmkvist, G.: Use-Cases: Patterns and Blueprints. Addison-Wesley (2005)

17. Rosenberg, D., Kendall, S.: Applying Use Case Driven Object Modeling with UML: an Annotated e-Commerce Example, 1st edn. Addison-Wesley, Boston (2001)

18. Santos, I., Andrade, R., Santos Neto, P.: Templates for textual use cases of software product lines: results from a systematic mapping study and a controlled experiment. J. Softw. Eng. Res. Dev. 3, 5 (2015). https://doi.org/10.1186/s40411-015-0020-3

19. Thakur, J., Gupta, A.: Automatic generation of sequence diagram from use case specification. In: Proceedings 7th India Software Engineering Conference, pp. 1–6. Association for Computing Machinery, New York, NY, USA (2014)

20. Yue, T., Briand, L., Labiche, Y.: A systematic review of transformation approaches between user requirements and analysis models. Requirements Eng. 16, 75–99 (2011). https://link.springer.com/article/10.1007/s00766-010-0111-y

Nexus Between Psychological Safety and Non-Technical Debt in Large-Scale Agile Enterprise Resource Planning Systems Development

Muhammad Ovais Ahmad[1]([⊠]) [iD] and Tomas Gustavsson[2] [iD]

[1] Department of Computer Science, Karlstad University, 651 88 Karlstad, Sweden
Ovais.ahmad@kau.se
[2] Karlstad Business School, Karlstad University, 651 88 Karlstad, Sweden
Tomas.gustavsson@kau.se

Abstract. Psychological safety, a pivotal factor in team dynamics, has been proposed as a crucial determinant of success in agile software development (ASD) teams and learning. However, the extent of its influence within the domain of large-scale agile (LSA) software development teams remains underexplored. This research investigates the multifaceted dimensions of psychological safety within LSA teams, examining both its precursors and outcomes. This study conducted semi-structured interviews with software professionals actively involved in LSA projects within a Swedish software consultancy company. The findings underscore the intricate nature of establishing a psychologically safe environment within LSA teams, revealing it as a multidimensional construct necessitating a proactive leadership approach, fostering open communication, and cultivating an ecosystem of constructive feedback. The study highlights the critical importance of intentionally shaping teams to facilitate continuous learning, ensuring remuneration safety, and implementing a comprehensive onboarding process for incoming team members. By fostering psychologically safe settings, LSA teams enhanced teamwork dynamics, heightened job satisfaction, and facilitation continuous learning and development. Notably, the absence of such an environment exacerbates the phenomenon of brain drain, exposing the tangible consequences of overlooking this fundamental aspect of organizational culture. This study proposes avenues for future research directions, aiming to further unravel the nuances of psychological safety and its cascading effects within the realm of contemporary LSA software development context.

Keywords: Psychological safety · Non-technical debt · Agile · Large-scale · Software development · ERP

1 Introduction

Agile methodologies enable software companies to enhance product quality and optimize customer value while concurrently facilitating rapid response to defects, improved communication, and effective coordination [2–5]. Nevertheless, these methodologies

A. Jarzębowicz et al. (Eds.): KKIO 2023, LNBIP 499, pp. 63–81, 2024.
https://doi.org/10.1007/978-3-031-51075-5_3

present distinct management challenges, some stemming from the consistent and essential communication needed for Agile practices to be effective. As clarified by Boehm and Turner [35], Agile methodologies bring diverse challenges encompassing conflicts within development processes, business procedures, and personnel dynamics. Central to the Agile approach is the foundation of collaborative relationships and interconnectedness among team members. It is important that any reservations team members harbor regarding potential outcomes of expressing their viewpoints – whether pertaining to identifying gaps in others' work or tackling difficulties in their tasks – do not impede overall performance. To enhance productivity, it is crucial to have an understanding of factors that impact the performance of both individuals and teams. Moreover, fostering an environment in which team members feel secure to propose ideas, acknowledge mistakes, seek assistance, or deliver feedback within hierarchies is equally critical [34, 48].

Psychological safety emerges as a crucial factor within teams operating in agile environments, particularly in the context of knowledge-intensive software tasks [1–3]. Psychological safety is defined as *"a shared belief held by members of a team that the team is safe for interpersonal risk-taking"* [6]. While agile software development (ASD) methodologies were tailored for small-scale projects, their potential positive outcomes have drawn interest in the context of Large-Scale Agile (LSA) software development projects.

The systematic literature reviews by Kalenda et al. [5] and Dikert et al. [4] highlighted various factors contributing to LSA success (e.g., management support, executive sponsorship, and teamwork support) and challenges (e.g., agile implementation difficulties, coordination complexities in multi-team settings, ambiguous roles of mid-level managers, pressure to deliver, and lack of knowledge and training) [4, 5]. These challenges also lead to various technical and non-technical debt in software projects [2]. Non-technical debt (NTD) encapsulates social, process-related, and human-related aspects of software development [2, 4, 5, 8]. To mitigate such challenges it is important that agile teams engage in open communication, foster strong collaborative relationships among team members, and that management offers a learning environment. Here, the concept of psychological safety emerges as a cornerstone of the agile team environment.

Psychological safety has been extensively studied within the realms of social science [3, 7–9], and its role in organizational research [3, 10]. Psychological safety exerts positive impacts on team performance, job satisfaction, and team reflexivity [3, 8, 11]. While limited research has explored psychological safety within Agile Software Development (ASD) settings [33], its specific implications within the context of LSA projects remain relatively unexplored [8]. To address this research gap, our study aims to answer the following research question:

• RQ: How does the relationship between psychological safety and non-technical debt manifest in LSA project environments?

The remainder of this paper is organised as follows: In Sect. 2, we provide information on related works and background to the LSA, debt in software and psychological safety. Section 3 presents our research setting, data collection, and analysis. Sections 4 and 5 present the results, and a validity discussion. Sections 6 and 7 offer discussions, conclusions, and future research directions, respectively.

2   Background

In this section, we provide an overview of three key sub-sections LSA, technical and non-technical debt, and psychological safety.

2.1   Large-Scale Agile

ASD represents a collection of iterative and incremental approaches with a focus on team collaboration, functional software delivery, responsiveness to customer needs, and adaptability to change [12]. These approaches are implemented in both small and large-scale software development projects [4, 5]. It is commonly advised to assemble agile teams comprising around 5 to 9 individuals [44]. This is suggested to enhance teamwork effectiveness by diminishing the number of communication connections. According to Williams and Cockburn [43] "....*the agile value set and practices best suit co-located teams of about 50 people or fewer who have easy access to user and business experts and are developing projects that are not life-critical.*" When a project necessitates more people, the responsibilities are allocated across multiple teams. This is often referred to as large-scale agile [44] and is defined as: "*Large-scale denote software development organizations with 50 or more people or at least six teams*" [4]. Dingsøyr, Fægri1, and Itkonen [44] propose a taxonomy for the scale of agile software development organizations which is summarized in the following Table 1.

Table 1. Taxonomy of scale of agile software development organizations, adopted from [44].

Level	Number of teams	Coordination approaches
Small-scale	1	Coordinating the team can be done using agile practices such as daily meetings, joint planning, reviews and retrospective meetings
Large-scale	2–9	Coordination of teams can be achieved in new forums such as Scrum of Scrums
Very large-scale	10 +	Several forums are needed for coordination, such as multiple Scrum of Scrums

The research on scaling ASD has grown considerably [4, 5, 49–52]. Several LSA frameworks such as LeSS, SAFe, DAD, Spotify, Nexus, and Scrum-at-Scale have been used in software companies. Organizations increasingly adopt these LSA frameworks, methods and processes to remain competitive in a rapidly changing environment. However, LSA projects are more complex than small-scale projects due to the increased number of stakeholders, dependencies, and technical challenges. The success of large-scale agile projects depends on the organization's ability to manage this complexity effectively.

Kalenda et al. [5] conducted a literature review and an action research study to identify practices, challenges, and success factors in scaling agile in large organizations. The reported key success factors for scaling agile are company culture, prior agile and lean experiences, management support, and incremental adoption, whereas the challenging factors are an overly aggressive roll-out time frame, resistance to change, and integration into preexisting non-agile business processes [5].

In the same vein, Dikert et al. [4] conducted a systematic literature review where a total of 52 papers were analysed on LSA transformations. The study identifies 35 reported challenges, and the most common ones include difficulty in implementing agile methods, integrating agile methods with other organizational processes, change resistance, lack of management support, and lack of skills and training [4]. The study also identifies 29 success factors, and the most common factors include management support, choosing and customizing the agile model, training and coaching, mindset and alignment, frequent constructive communication, and collaboration [4].

To summarise, teams operating within the LSA context encounter numerous challenges (e.g., managing intricate interdependencies, diverse team compositions, roles, and personalities, suboptimal processes, conflicting priorities among teams, and complex and ambiguous objectives) [4, 5, 13], which give rise to Non-technical Debt [2, 14].

2.2 Technical and Non-Technical Debt

Technical Debt (TD) refers to a metaphor coined by Cunningham [39], which symbolizes the adoption of design or implementation approaches that may not be ideal initially but offer short-term advantages. These choices can lead to increased costs or even feasibility challenges when making changes over the medium to long term [41]. The effective management of such suboptimal strategies is crucial for software companies. The existence of TD is an inevitable reality and can even be advantageous under specific circumstances [40–42]. These circumstances often stem from unpredictable internal or external business or environmental factors that the organization faces. In the literature, there are different types of technical debt (e.g. architectural debt, code debt, test debt, defect debt) and non-technical debt (e.g. process debt, people debt, social debt, organisational debt) [2, 42]. TD is extensively studied and there are several explanation of the phenomenon, such as:

- *"The debt incurred through the speeding up of software project development which results in several deficiencies ending up in high maintenance overheads"* [39].
- *"A design or construction approach that is expedient in the short term but that creates a technical context in which the same work will cost more to do later than it would cost to do now"* [40].
- *"A collection of design or implementation constructs that are expedient in the short term, but set up a technical context that can make future changes more costly or impossible. TD presents an actual or contingent liability whose impact is limited to internal system qualities, primarily maintainability and evolvability"* [41].

The current state-of-the-art practices in software engineering recommend mitigating TD by avoiding it when its consequences are known or refactoring or rewriting code and other artifacts to remove accumulated suboptimal solutions and their negative impact. Lenarduzzi et al. [42] conducted a systematic review of technical debt prioritization in the following areas: strategies, processes, factors, and tools. The review identified 44 primary studies and found that there is no single, agreed-upon approach to technical debt prioritization.

Another systematic review [2] investigates the concept of NTD in software engineering, which is defined as the debt that is incurred when social, process, and people issues. The review reported several NTD causes and mitigation strategies. However, the results show that NTD is often overlooked, but that it can have a significant impact on the success of a software project [2].

Process debt is defined as *"a sub-optimal activity or process that might have short-term benefits but generates a negative impact in the medium-long term."* [2]. Process debt arises when organizations overlook the development of process competence, experience process divergence, and become entangled in uncontrolled external dependencies [2].

"Social debt is a cumulative and increasing cost in the current state of things, connected to invisible and negative effects within a development community" [2]. Social debt stems from gender biases, deficient communication and collaboration, hierarchical power dynamics, organizational silos, lack of empathy and so on [2].

Personnel-related debt mainly emerges due to rigid team members, demotivation among junior members, inadequately informed management decisions, and an absence of psychosocial safety [2]. Most of these issues revolve around people-centric or contextual concerns.

2.3 Psychological Safety

Psychological safety refers to a collective perception held by team members that the company provides a secure environment for them to take interpersonal risks. It is a sought-after attribute within agile organizations, as it correlates with principles like equitable employee participation, reduced hierarchical power dynamics, and enhanced organisational learning. These principles are often exemplified by the flatter organizational structures commonly found in agile settings. Psychological safety is defined as *"a shared belief held by members of a team that the team is safe for interpersonal risk-taking"* [6]. In simpler terms, psychological safety embodies a feeling of trust and inclusion that empowers team members to confidently take risks and express their thoughts without worrying about criticism or reprisals. This, in turn, can result in heightened levels of innovation, communication, collaboration, and overall productivity.

Psychological safety has a moderating impact on communication gaps and collaboration challenges, whereas the extent of collaboration linked to task-based activities exhibits both encouraging and mitigating outcomes [2]. In LSA, the complexity highlights the need for greater collaboration among employees and teams. However, this can negatively impact individual software engineers when their ideas lead to unexpected results, potentially hindering both personal and organizational development. To address this, fostering a safe work environment where employees feel free to propose ideas, provide honest feedback, take risks, and experiment becomes crucial. A positive correlation exists between the openness and transformational leadership displayed by managers and the level of psychological safety within teams [15]. Psychological safety plays a vital role in facilitating successful collaboration, open communication, knowledge and information sharing, and learning from failures and performance [6, 16–19]. Inter-team coordination does not correlate significantly with team performance, but psychological safety displays a notably strong positive relationship with team performance [7].

However, social agile practices (e.g., daily scrums, retrospectives, pair programming) exert a positive influence on psychological safety, transparency, communication, and productivity [20]. To cultivate a psychologically safe environment, it is essential to establish a collective sense of responsibility for team performance [21, 22]. According to Edmondson [6], there is a positive influence of team psychological safety on team performance, which is mediated by team learning behaviour.

For the individual, Safdar et al. [11] demonstrate that psychological safety significantly impacts a software engineer's choice of knowledge sources. A software engineer who perceives a high level of psychological safety is more inclined to seek input from team members, whereas a software engineer experiencing lower psychological safety tends to rely on external sources [11].

Lenberg and Feldt [3] investigated the relationship between psychological safety and norm clarity in software engineering teams. The authors [3] conducted a survey of 217 software developers in 38 development teams working for five different organizations investigating psychological safety, team norm clarity, team performance, and job satisfaction. Their results showed that both psychological safety and team norm clarity were correlated with team performance and job satisfaction.

Alami, Zahedi, and Krancher [33] explored how psychological safety materializes in agile software development teams. The authors surveyed with 365 respondents and 18 interviewees with software professionals. Their results show that in the context of ASD, the institutionalization of psychological safety necessitates collaborative efforts from individuals, teams, and leadership to implement strategies for blame-free, open, and collective decision-making within the team, actively fostering a psychologically safe environment [33].

Tkalich et al. [45] examined the impact of remote work on psychological safety in software engineering teams. Their results offer three essential recommendations. Firstly, teams should emphasize the importance of onsite collaboration and spontaneous interactions. Secondly, it's advised to align work arrangements within teams or consider restructuring them to create groups of like-minded individuals. Lastly, teams should explore the adoption of institutionalized norms that encourage behaviours conducive to psychological safety. These steps collectively contribute to the development of a work environment where team members feel safe to express themselves and take risks without fear of judgment or reprisal.

According to Thorgren and Caiman [37], psychological safety is indispensable for the successful implementation of agile practices in cross-cultural teams. Nurturing psychological safety within a team, potential conflicts and tensions arising from the intersection of agile practices, values, and organizational culture can be mitigated [37]. Hennel and Rosenkranz [20] findings suggest that social Agile practices (e.g., daily standups, retrospectives, and Sprint planning) influence psychological safety, transparency, communication, and ultimately, productivity [20].

More recently, Verwijs and Russo [28] conducted a study with 1118 participants from 161 teams to explore how diversity, conflict, and psychological safety impact agile software teams. Their results show that the presence of age diversity within a team has a beneficial impact on team effectiveness, while gender diversity tends to lead to increased relational conflict. Furthermore, psychological safety directly contributes to improved teamwork and reduced conflict within the team. However, it's important to note that psychological safety does not act as a moderator in influencing the relationship between diversity and team effectiveness. Ahmad [8] explored the antecedents and effects of psychological safety on LSA teams and reported that a proactive leadership approach, open communication, and constructive feedback are key contributing factors to offering a psychologically safe environment.

3 Research Settings

The grounded theory (GT) approach comprises a series of steps encompassing data collection, analysis, formulation of theoretical constructs, and reporting [23]. GT enables researchers to detect recurring patterns within interview transcripts by consistently contrasting data at varying levels of abstraction [24]. Unlike relying on preconceived hypotheses, this approach seeks to reveal the concerns expressed by interviewees throughout the process. This study centered on comprehending the LSA development experience, challenges within the work environment, and strategies employed in real-world scenarios.

Semi-structured interviews were conducted with seven agile practitioners from a consultancy company in Sweden. The chosen case company participates in the NODLA project, utilizing diverse agile methods in its software development projects. The NODLA project, funded by the Knowledge Foundation in Sweden, aims to investigate NTD, causes leading to the accumulation of NTD, impacts of NTD, and mitigation strategies in the context of large-scale ASD. Our case company develops and offers consultancy services in ERP Systems, Business Insights, and Integrations. The case company is a leading technology services provider for Scandinavian food companies.

Semi-structured interviews were conducted via the Zoom application and ranged from 1 to 2 h in duration. The interviewees held various roles, with some having multiple responsibilities. Table 2 illustrates the diverse roles, including software developers, project managers, Scrum masters, and business analysts. Four of the seven participants possessed over five years of experience, while the remaining three had 1 to 3 years of experience.

All participants in the study had hands-on experience with agile methodologies. The interview questions were organized around four main areas: professional background, agile practices within their teams, communication and collaboration practices, and the team environment. Each transcript underwent meticulous analysis involving line-by-line examination to identify key points. These points were documented as open codes, undergoing iterative comparison throughout the analysis. Such techniques enable researchers to assess and contrast new codes against those previously identified [23].

4 Results

The outcomes of this study are organized into four distinct sub-sections. Firstly, the study underscores the significance of leaders' behaviour as a crucial precursor to fostering an environment of psychological safety. Secondly, it emphasizes the pivotal role of leaders

Table 2. Interviewees' background.

ID	Interviewee's title	Experience
E1	Developer – Integration Specialist	1 year
E2	Project Manager	2 years
E3	Scrum Master	7 years
E4	Developer – with multiple roles	20 years
E5	Manager	10 years
E6	Scrum master	5 years
E7	Business analyst – with multiple roles	3 years

in forming teams that prioritize learning. Thirdly, the study underscores the necessity of cultivating trustworthy and respectful interpersonal connections both within and beyond LSA teams. Lastly, the findings illuminate that a lack of psychological safety within an organization results in talent attrition, underscoring the repercussions of neglecting this vital facet of organizational culture. Figure 1 illustrates that leadership behaviour is an enabler for a psychologically safe environment, as well as its potential effect on individuals and teams within the context of LSA projects.

4.1 Leadership Role

The creation of a psychologically safe work environment largely depends on leadership behaviour, which is essential for building a setting where people feel free to share their thoughts without fear of punishment. This dynamic synergy between leaders and the team's psychological well-being fosters an environment of open expression and mutual respect.

A senior manager emphasized on the significance of balance, drawing a comparison between leadership roles in facilitating a harmonious synergy between two essential factors: ensuring customer satisfaction and promoting employee contentment. Further, the respondent emphasizes the importance of cultivating an "agility mindset" as a key strategy. This mindset is instrumental in ensuring that not only are customers satisfied but that the organization consistently delivers value to all its stakeholders. It highlights the intricate balance between employee well-being and customer satisfaction as central to the company's philosophy and strategic approach.

"Our top focus is to be a great place to work at and to have happy employees and at the same time, be a customer-centric organisation. That's where the agility mindset comes into play because if we have happy customers, then we normally deliver good value to our other stakeholders" (E5).

In this safe setting, people have the mental freedom to openly share their concerns and viewpoints. In such an environment, the push to communicate comes from a lack of perceived barriers and a heightened sense of psychological security. Interviewee E2 shares insights into this dynamic and that they have not observed pervasive fear of

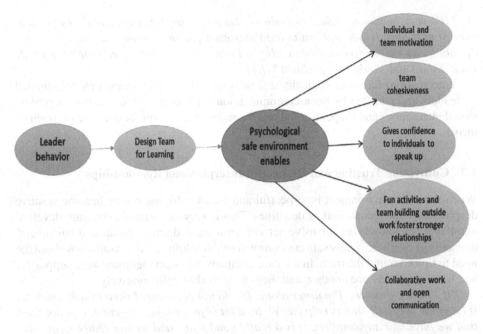

Fig. 1. Conceptual map of factors that enable psychological safe environment and its effects

expressing dissenting opinions or concerns within the workplace. Instead, the interviewee suggests that individuals within the organization do feel comfortable speaking their minds when they encounter issues or discontent. This insight sheds light on the organization's environment, suggesting a degree of openness and willingness to engage in constructive dialogue when addressing concerns or disagreements.

"I haven't felt at least that people are afraid to speak their minds because people do speak their minds if they are unhappy with something" (E2).

When a psychologically safe environment exists, its endeavours extend beyond professional realms, allowing for shared fun activities. Such activities strengthen the foundation of interpersonal bonds and underpin the cohesiveness of the team. Such a confluence of social interaction within an organizational context emerges as a nurturing ground for collaboration:

"We do a lot of things together, like [when we're] *off work and stuff. So, it's fun"* (E1).

The interviewees provide valuable insight into their perspective on the importance of self-reflection and continuous improvement within the organization. They emphasize the value of consistently evaluating their actions and outcomes with the intention of identifying opportunities for enhancement. However, the journey towards fostering this psychological safety is not without challenges. An interviewee sheds light on the feelings of hesitation that may be covering the act of admitting mistakes or acknowledging performance issues. This disclosure dilemma underscores the underlying psychological complexities of admitting vulnerability in a professional context:

"It's very helpful to reflect and always keep in mind what we can do better and change next time. It is a problem to tell the truth if [there is] something that you think did not go as well as you wanted to. Maybe I can be a little bit scared to tell the whole truth. I think that could be a problem" (E1).

The creation of a psychologically safe workspace is a sophisticated link coordinated by leaders and nurtured by open communication. This delicate balance boosts professional interactions and shapes a collaborative and secure environment where individuals thrive.

4.2 Cultivating Trusting and Respectful Interpersonal Relationships

When the work environment is respectful and trustworthy, the results become positive despite strict time constraints or deadlines. This is very important in software development as it is a knowledge-intensive activity with many discussions around customers' demands. A psychologically safe environment enables difficult conversations without the need to tiptoe around the truth. In the case company, the team members were supportive and helpful towards one another, and they often worked collaboratively:

"If I have a problem, I'm never alone. If I do not act alone, I need to ask someone. If I do that, they will always help me. We do a lot of funny things together. I do not think that we have had any conflicts. It is a really good team, and we are really supporting and lifting up each other. So, I think that everyone can see that our team is very friendly" (E4).

It can also be a sign of team cohesiveness when everyone works towards the same goal. It is noteworthy that being friendly does not mean that professional activities are overlooked. Listening to each team member's opinions is essential to avoid conflicts, as an interviewee explained:

"…[a] friendly team is something that we do not have to be too much friends with. We question each other and listen to each other's opinions. I think that is one of the reasons why we do not have this conflict. We are very friendly and we don't want to fire our voices if that can lead to a conflict" (E4).

Furthermore, it is important that meetings and discussions at the workplace should not be only work-related. It should also offer an opportunity for team members to connect and engage with one another on a social level. The interviewees emphasize the significance of interpersonal dynamics beyond the realm of professional responsibilities. Interviewee E3 emphasizes the fusion of professional and social elements and suggests that a satisfying and healthy work environment is one where both aspects are carefully considered and nurtured.

"Suppose there are problems, how people tell if they're satisfied and if they're ill or something. So it's just like a social meeting as well, not just work" (E3).

Building and keeping a strong team spirit involves a mix of creating a friendly atmosphere and sticking to professional values. This mix is improved by bringing together important things like open communication, mutual support, and considering everyone's different viewpoints. When these things work well together, they create a close and cooperative team that contributes positively to both individual and collective success.

4.3 Brain Drain

The phenomenon known as "brain drain" within the context of organizational dynamics pertains to the leaving of employees driven by a variety of factors, which can include challenging work conditions, insufficient intrinsic motivation, inadequate remuneration, and a lack of psychological safety. The ability to attract and keep highly skilled employees may be influenced by offering competitive pay, providing a safe and supportive work setting, and fostering a team-oriented corporate culture.

"To be brutally honest, I know that some people left last year because they thought that they weren't getting paid enough" (E2).

It is rational to posit that employees who perceive psychological safety and fair compensation are more inclined to maintain their allegiance to the company. The departure of a proficient employee echoes immediately within the team, impacting both the collective performance and individual work. This was underscored by an interviewee who highlighted a skill gap resulting from a departed colleague:

"He was a really good programmer, and we miss him a bit" (E6).

Moreover, the financial aspect, though significant, is not the sole determinant of employee resignations. The decision to leave stems from a multifaceted interplay of factors encompassing the nature of work, the work environment, and personal considerations. A senior team member sheds light on this complex dynamic as:

"One of the reasons that I've heard is that it's about the salary. That is important, and [the income] *can differ if we live here* [a Scandinavian country's capital] *permanently as well.* [The reasons for quitting] *can depend on a lot of things. Some of my closest colleagues and I discuss. Sometimes, it feels like* [employees] *leave* [after just a short time]. *They understand things differently than what has actually happened to them"* (E4).

When developers lack an internal impetus or genuine interest in their tasks, retaining their commitment becomes a challenge. Intrinsic motivation, deriving from activities that individuals inherently find enjoyable or stimulating, goes beyond external rewards. Several interviewees highlighted the absence of engaging tasks as a factor contributing to dissatisfaction. For instance, an interviewee expressed the situation as:

"A risk or a factor [is] *that people want to live. It is not fun to have too much* [work] *to do and no fun* [activities] *to do; actually* [it is] *always tricky"* (E1).

Employee turnover is a pivotal topic within the realm of organizational behaviour and human resource management. Understanding the underlying reasons behind employees leaving an organization is essential for both retention efforts and the overall well-being of the workforce. Employees depart due to factors that transcend the company itself and relate more to their personal career aspirations and preferences. Interviewee E7 highlights a prevalent and intriguing reason for employee departures – the attraction of another job offer that aligns with their personal career aspirations. These decisions are often unrelated to any shortcomings within their current organization but rather driven by the prospect of working on projects or roles that hold deeper personal significance.

"The most common reason is that they get another job offer on something they really want to work with. It has nothing to do with our company. It's more like they're going to work with something they appreciate more" (E7).

The interviewees further provide valuable perspective on how certain employees perceive and react to fluctuations in their workloads. They describe a phenomenon where employees become "addicted" to project-driven work, with periods of high activity followed by extended phases of relative inactivity. An integration specialist elaborated that dissatisfaction with work conditions and the lack of tasks contribute to employees' decisions to resign:

"They think that the conditions are not good enough. [They] are addicted to having projects; maybe like some months, they have much to do. And then for half a year, it's hard to get projects that they're used to, so they don't have much to do, and they feel under-stimulated and like, 'I want a new job so I can have more tasks to do'" (E1).

In a nutshell, brain drain encapsulates a range of intricately intertwined factors that precipitate developers' resignation. Effective retention strategies necessitate a comprehensive approach that addresses remuneration, psychological safety, stimulating work environments, and opportunities for professional growth. The interplay of these factors can significantly influence the decision of skilled employees to stay committed to an organization.

4.4 Designing a Team for Learning

Organisations need to develop the idea of designing teams for learning, which involves multiple factors such as an efficient onboarding process, creating a culture of continuous learning and knowledge sharing, reflection and feedback. The starting point for designing a team for learning is to identify the competence development gap and a good onboarding process for new employees. A point of caution in the onboarding process is whom to involve and when to be involved. When the process includes only senior members of the company, it becomes stressful for them. Two interviewees expressed this situation as follows:

"We have found that in the management team with the overall responsibility for competence development, that kind of role is sort of missing at the moment. We were working with scaled agile. We had to fill in who would be responsible for each role, and we saw that overall competence development was lacking. We have an operation manager who is leading operations but maybe not clearly responsible for competence development" (E5).

"Onboarding is a big issue that we have to work with and maybe not just talk about it. We have to take care of the people who are here and remain with a nice spirit. I think that it is important because if we get bigger and bigger, it puts a lot of pressure on senior consultants, and we have to be careful of them" (E3).

Software development is a knowledge-intensive activity, where knowledge sharing is an important element. The effective dissemination of knowledge and experiences among team members not only bolsters problem-solving capabilities but also promotes collaboration and innovation. A Scrum master expressed positive experiences about their psychologically safe environment for sharing knowledge:

"We have quite recently started knowledge-sharing sessions. One person in our team is responsible for administering these meetings and setting up the agenda. So, we are starting to work with it … in our sprint planning to have knowledge sharing and talk

about how we can do things better. It's an initiative from me or my colleagues who are the value-stream managers" (E3).

The Scrum masters highlight that the recently started knowledge-sharing sessions are an initiative from the team members themselves, which is significant. Within the team, one person is responsible for administering these meetings. This shows that the team is committed to making knowledge sharing a priority. Along with various work practices, the interviewees highlighted that good communication platforms (e.g., Slack, Microsoft Teams, etc.) for internal communication and social interaction are also essential.

5 Threats to Validity and Limitations

We collected the data from interviews with software professionals from a Swedish software consultancy company. All the codes and concepts were directly obtained from the interviews. Our findings are sufficiently grounded in the substantive data [23] but cannot be generalized on a large scale due to the limited number of participants. Therefore, caution should be taken when applying these results to other software companies. The inherent limitation of the GT is that it is only based on a particular investigative context [25].

James and Busher [26] highlighted the risk regarding the authenticity of the participants in digital interviews. We were confident that all the participants were interviewed with the permission of the company representative and with a signed NDA. In this way, such risks are mitigated in this study. The GT approach used in this study involved subjective interpretation of the data. The findings and the emerging concepts presented in this study are based on the researchers' interpretation of the data, which may differ from other researchers' interpretations. Despite these limitations, this study's findings offer valuable insights into psychological safety, leadership, and NTD in LSA development. The concepts are sufficiently supported with quotations from the participants' interviews, and the findings are discussed in detail and characterized by some existing concepts.

6 Discussion

This study explores the antecedents and effects of psychological safety within LSA teams. The results suggest that building a psychologically safe environment is a multidimensional challenge that requires a proactive leadership approach, a competent team design focused on learning, open communication and feedback, remuneration safety, and a well-prepared onboarding process for new team members. These factors contribute to effective teamwork, work satisfaction, and learning, as well as promoting a psychologically safe and collaborative learning environment.

One of the key findings of this research is the pivotal role of proactive leadership in fostering psychological safety. To create a more psychologically safe environment, leaders and management should show appreciation for employees [19] and provide opportunities for their involvement in projects so that they can learn from their mistakes and failures. The guidance and behaviour of leaders play a crucial role in creating an environment where team members feel secure in expressing their opinions and concerns without fear of retribution. While leadership is undeniably pivotal, other organizational elements, such as established workflows, shared values, and organizational strategies, also contribute to fostering a safe workspace. Therefore, the 'agility mindset' emerges not merely as a leadership strategy but as an organizational ethos that balances both employee well-being and customer satisfaction. While multiple studies in the realm of social sciences demonstrate that psychological safety cultivates learning-oriented actions like soliciting feedback, experimentation, and deliberation of mistakes [6, 9], its pivotal role in LSA has not been recognized.

The management needs to identify competence gaps and design teams for learning. It is important that teams are designed in a way that prioritizes learning. Edmondson [6] highlighted the importance of psychosocial safety and its impact on team learning and team performance [6]. Teams structured to facilitate continuous learning and skill development are more likely to promote psychological safety, as team members perceive their growth as a shared objective. In a software development project, team cohesion magnifies the impact of psychological safety on knowledge sharing [27]. Psychological safety directly contributes to effectiveness [28].

On the other hand, the lack of psychological safety contributes to social and people debt [8, 14], whereas a high level of psychological safety has significant positive correlations to LSA team performance [7], the success of process innovations [17], and mitigating effects of the lack of both communication and collaboration [8]. It is also important to design teams for learning and have a well-prepared onboarding process for new employees. It is vital to know whom to involve and when to involve senior team members because it builds pressure on senior consultants and creates the need to take care of existing teams while remaining focused on making the company to excel.

Agile teams strive for continuous improvement through recurrent feedback and introspection [38]. Psychological safety cultivates an environment wherein team constituents are enabled to provide and accept valuable feedback and facilitate learning [34]. Transparent communication and constructive feedback mechanisms emerged as vital components of a psychologically safe environment. The ability to express ideas openly and the presence of feedback loops contribute to a sense of security, enabling team members to share their perspectives and learn from their mistakes without apprehension. Detert and Burris [15] revealed a positive correlation between the managers' openness and transformational leadership with psychological safety. It is also evident that providing room for reflection and open feedback is important; otherwise, individuals or teams will hide their real troublesome situations. High-quality interpersonal relationships among the team members enhance their psychological safety, leading to positive and effective learning [16, 32] and sharing behaviours [29].

Our results show that trusting and respectful interpersonal relationships in LSA teams help avoid conflicts and prepare a breeding ground for a safe and collaborative learning environment. Dreesen et al. [14] and Ahmad et al. [2] reported that a lack of psychological safety in software development might contribute to social debt. A key manifestation of high-quality relationships is relational coordination, along with shared goals, shared knowledge, and mutual respect [30, 31]. Relational coordination is defined as "*a mutually reinforcing process of interaction between communication and relationships carried out for the purpose of task integration*" [30] (p. 301). This is more important in software development as this knowledge-intensive activity requires creativity in solving a particular problem and completing a task. Balancing a formal work environment with strong personal connections is challenging for organizations, especially in fields that require specialized knowledge such as software development. However, focusing on relational coordination would enable double-loop learning instead of single-loop learning in teams.

Our research highlighted the significance of remuneration safety – the assurance of fair compensation – as a factor influencing psychological safety. Employee retention cannot be boiled down to financial incentives alone. The subtleties of work culture, the nature of the work itself, and personal aspirations also play into the equation. This underlines the importance of recognizing employees' value and contributions in cultivating a conducive atmosphere. The study encourages us to evaluate how effective money-based retention strategies really are and to consider if a more comprehensive approach that includes psychological safety might yield better results in keeping employees. An intriguing aspect brought to light by our findings is the impact of enjoyable social activities outside of work on team cohesion and conflict prevention. These activities not only strengthen relationships but also contribute to a more cohesive and harmonious team dynamic. By encouraging a sense of friendship and shared experiences, such activities create a platform for open interaction and contribute to a more psychologically secure environment.

7 Conclusion

This study highlights the significance of psychological safety in LSA teams. The findings emphasize that psychological safety is an intricate construct deeply embedded within the organizational culture, influenced by leadership behavior, interpersonal relationships, and the very nature of work. Therefore, adopting a holistic approach that considers these complex interactions would be beneficial for organizations. The establishment of a safe and supportive environment for team members has far-reaching effects on various aspects of team performance and dynamics. A psychologically safe environment has been shown to positively influence confidence, collaboration, communication, motivation, and overall job satisfaction. Moreover, our research underscores that psychological safety is not an isolated factor but is intricately connected with other factors of effective teamwork. Open communication, feedback mechanisms, proactive leadership, and equitable remuneration collectively contribute to the fostering of psychological safety and developer retention. In this regard, it's worth noting that psychological safety does not imply a lack of challenges or conflicts. Rather, it provides a framework within which conflicts can be constructively addressed without fear of negative consequences.

8 Future Research Directions

The insights gained from this study pave the way for several promising avenues for future research. First, a notable area of exploration is the examination of the relationship between organizational culture, employee diversity, and psychological safety. Understanding how different cultural contexts and diverse teams influence the dynamics of psychological safety could provide valuable insights into its nuanced nature.

Second, investigation is warranted into the reasons behind the departure of knowledgeable team members. Exploring strategies to retain such members while ensuring their continued growth and learning could be instrumental in enhancing team performance and stability.

Third, research could delve deeper into the design of teams for learning. Effective methods for assessing individual and team competencies and strategies for fostering continuous learning deserve more attention. Furthermore, the role of reflective practices and open feedback in nurturing psychological safety warrants in-depth exploration.

Fourth, beyond psychological safety, other contextual factors, such as remote work arrangements, intrinsic motivation, and the geographical proximity of workplaces, could impact team dynamics. Investigating these factors and their interactions could provide valuable insights for enhancing employee satisfaction and overall team effectiveness.

Fifth, exploring the effects of gender distribution on psychological safety would be interesting to investigate, as gender biases contribute to NTD [2].

Sixth, in addition to investigating the concept of psychological safety, it would be worthwhile to explore the role of social and task-related factors as moderators. The categorization elaboration model [46], serves as a valuable framework for such research due to its capacity to integrate and reconcile the contrasting mechanisms of diversity postulated by cognitive resource diversity theory and the similarity-attraction paradigm.

From a practical standpoint, this will stimulate the development of training programs and methodologies aimed at assisting teams and organizations in capitalizing on their diversity across various dimensions. This extends beyond traditional categories like gender, age, cultural background, and functional roles. Moreover, it is crucial to direct increased attention toward the beliefs held by teams regarding diversity and its potential impacts. The concept of a "Diversity Mind-Set" as elaborated by Van Knippenberg and Schippers [47], can serve as a moderator by fostering team awareness of their diversity and its capacity to enrich their collective team experience.

In conclusion, this study's findings emphasize the significance of a psychologically safe environment in nurturing positive team dynamics, learning, and performance. As we look ahead, future research has immense potential to delve deeper into these dynamics and explore their impacts on various facets of software development and LSA teams' effectiveness.

Acknowledgement. This work was supported by the Knowledge Foundation, Sweden, through the NODLA project and Helge Ax:son Johnsons Stiftelse.

References

1. Beecham, S., Baddoo, N., Hall, T., Robinson, H., Sharp, H.: Motivation in software engineering: a systematic literature review. Inf. Softw. Technol. **50**(9–10), 860–878 (2008)
2. Ahmad, M.O., Gustavsson, T.: The pandora's box of social, process, and people debts in software engineering. J. Software Evol. Process (2022). https://doi.org/10.1002/smr.2516
3. Lenberg, P., Feldt, R.: Psychological safety and norm clarity in software engineering teams. In: Proceedings of the 11th International Workshop on Cooperative and Human Aspects of Software Engineering (2018)

4. Dikert, K., Paasivaara, M., Lassenius, C.: Challenges and success factors for large-scale agile transformations: a systematic literature review. J. Syst. Softw. **119**, 87–108 (2016). https://doi.org/10.1016/j.jss.2016.06.013

5. Kalenda, M., Hyna, P., Rossi, B.: Scaling agile in large organizations: Practices, challenges, and success factors. J. Software Evol. Process **30**(10), e1954 (2018)

6. Edmondson, A.: Psychological safety and learning behavior in work teams. Adm. Sci. Q. **44**(2), 350–383 (1999)

7. Gustavsson, T.: Team performance in large-scale agile software development. In: Insfran, E., González, F., Abrahão, S., Fernández, M., Barry, C., Lang, M., Linger, H., Schneider, C. (eds.) Advances in Information Systems Development. LNISO, vol. 55, pp. 237–254. Springer, Cham (2022). https://doi.org/10.1007/978-3-030-95354-6_14

8. Ahmad, M.O.: psychological safety, leadership and non-technical debt in large-scale agile software development. In: Proceedings of the 18th Conference on Computer Science and Intelligence Systems, pp. 327–334 (2023)

9. Newman, A., Donohue, R., Eva, N.: Psychological safety: a systematic review of the literature. Hum. Resour. Manag. Rev. **27**(3), 521–535 (2017)

10. Delizonna, L.: High-performing teams need psychological safety: here's how to create it (2017). https://hbr.org/2017/08/high-performing-teams-need-psychological-safety-heres-how-to-create-it

11. Safdar, U., Badir, Y.F., Afsar, B.: Who can I ask? how psychological safety affects knowledge sourcing among new product development team members. J. High Technol. Managem. Res. **28**(1), 79–92 (2017)

12. Manifesto, A.: Manifesto for agile software development (2001). https://agilemanifesto.org/

13. Edison, H., Wang, X., Conboy, K.: Comparing methods for large-scale agile software development: a systematic literature review. IEEE Trans. Software Eng. **48**(8), 2709–2731 (2021)

14. Dreesen, T., Hennel, P., Rosenkranz, C., Kude, T.: The second vice is lying, the first is running into debt. Antecedents and Mitigating Practices of Social Debt: An Exploratory Study in Distributed Software Development Teams. HICSSA. (2021)

15. Detert, J.R., Burris, E.R.: Leadership behavior and employee voice: is the door really open? Acad. Manag. J. **50**(4), 869–884 (2007)

16. Edmondson, A.C., Kramer, R.M., Cook, K.S.: Psychological safety, trust, and learning in organizations: a group-level lens. Trust Distrust Organ. Dilemmas Approaches **12**(2004), 239–272 (2004)

17. Baer, M., Frese, M.: Innovation is not enough: climates for initiative and psychological safety, process innovations, and firm performance. J. Organ. Behav. Int. J. Ind. Occup. Organ. Psychol. Behav. **24**(1), 45–68 (2003)

18. Carmeli, A., Gittell, J.H.: High-quality relationships, psychological safety, and learning from failures in work organizations. J. Organ. Behav. **30**(6), 709–729 (2009). https://doi.org/10.1002/job.565

19. Nembhard, I.M., Edmondson, A.C.: Making it safe: the effects of leader inclusiveness and professional status on psychological safety and improvement efforts in health care teams. J. Organ. Behav. Int. J. Ind. Occup. Organ. Psychol. Behav. **27**(7), 941–966 (2006)

20. Hennel, P., Rosenkranz, C.: Investigating the "Socio" in socio-technical development: the case for psychological safety in agile information systems development. Proj. Manag. J. **52**(1), 11–30 (2021)

21. Valentine, M.A., Edmondson, A.C.: Team scaffolds: how mesolevel structures enable role-based coordination in temporary groups. Organ. Sci. **26**(2), 405–422 (2015)

22. O'Neill, O.A.: Workplace expression of emotions and escalation of commitment 1. J. Appl. Soc. Psychol. **39**(10), 2396–2424 (2009)

23. Glaser, B.G.: Basics of Grounded Theory Analysis: Emergence vs Forcing. Sociology press (1992)
24. Stol, K.-J., Ralph, P., Fitzgerald, B.: Grounded theory in software engineering research: a critical review and guidelines. In: Proceedings of the 38th International Conference on Software Engineering, pp. 120–131 (2016)
25. Adolph, S., Kruchten, P.: Summary for scrutinizing agile practices or shoot-out at process corral! In: Companion of the 30th International Conference on Software engineering, pp. 1031–1032 (2008)
26. James, N., Busher, H.: Credibility, authenticity and voice: dilemmas in online interviewing. Qual. Res. **6**(3), 403–420 (2006)
27. Kakar, A.K.: How do team cohesion and psychological safety impact knowledge sharing in software development projects? Knowl. Process. Manag. **25**(4), 258–267 (2018)
28. Verwijs, C., Russo, D.: The double-edged sword of diversity: how diversity, conflict, and psychological safety impact agile software teams. arXiv preprint arXiv:2301.12954 (2023)
29. Carmeli, A., Brueller, D., Dutton, J.E.: Learning behaviours in the workplace: the role of high-quality interpersonal relationships and psychological safety. Syst. Res. Behav. Sci. Official J. Int. Fed. Syst. Res. **26**(1), 81–98 (2009)
30. Gittell, J.H.: A theory of relational coordination. In: Cameron, K.S., Dutton ve RE Quinn, J.E., (Ed.), Positive organizational scholarship: Foundations of a new discipline, pp. 279–295. San Francisco: Berrett-Koehler Publishers (2003)
31. Gittell, J.H.: Relational coordination: coordinating work through relationships of shared goals, shared knowledge and mutual respect. Relational Perspectives in Organizational Studies: A Research Companion, pp. 74–94 (2006)
32. Kahn, W.A.: Psychological conditions of personal engagement and disengagement at work. Acad. Manag. J. **33**(4), 692–724 (1990)
33. Alami, A., Zahedi, M., Krancher, O.: Antecedents of psychological safety in agile software development teams. Inf. Softw. Technol. **162**, 107267 (2023). https://doi.org/10.1016/j.infsof.2023.107267
34. Edmondson, A.C., Lei, Z.: Psychological safety: the history, renaissance, and future of an interpersonal construct. Annu. Rev. Organ. Psychol. Organ. Behav. **1**(1), 23–43 (2014)
35. Boehm, B., Turner, R.: Management challenges to implementing agile processes in traditional development organizations. IEEE Softw. **22**(5), 30–39 (2005)
36. Jehn, K.A., Mannix, E.A.: The dynamic nature of conflict: a longitudinal study of intragroup conflict and group performance. Acad. Manag. J. **44**(2), 238–251 (2001)
37. Thorgren, S., Caiman, E.: The role of psychological safety in implementing agile methods across cultures. Res. Technol. Manag. **62**(2), 31–39 (2019)
38. Alami, A., Krancher, O., Paasivaara, M.: The journey to technical excellence in agile software development. Inf. Softw. Technol. **150**, 106959 (2022)
39. Cunningham, W.: The WyCash portfolio management system. ACM Sigplan Oops Messenger **4**(2), 29–30 (1992)
40. McConnell, S.: Managing Technical Debt. Construx Software Builders, Inc., pp. 1–14 (2008)
41. Avgeriou, P., Kruchten, P., Nord, R.L., Ozkaya, I., Seaman, C.: Reducing friction in software development. IEEE Softw. **33**(1), 66–73 (2015)
42. Lenarduzzi, V., Besker, T., Taibi, D., Martini, A., Fontana, F.A.: A systematic literature review on technical debt prioritization: strategies, processes, factors, and tools. J. Syst. Softw. **171**, 110827 (2021)
43. Williams, L., Cockburn, A.: Agile software development: it's about feedback and change. Computer **36**(6), 39–43 (2003)

44. Dingsøyr, T., Fægri, T.E., Itkonen, J.: What Is large in large-scale? a taxonomy of scale for agile software development. In: Jedlitschka, A., Kuvaja, P., Kuhrmann, M., Männistö, T., Münch, J., Raatikainen, M. (eds.) PROFES 2014. LNCS, vol. 8892, pp. 273–276. Springer, Cham (2014). https://doi.org/10.1007/978-3-319-13835-0_20

45. Tkalich, A., Šmite, D., Andersen, N.H., Moe, N.B.: What happens to psychological safety when going remote?. IEEE Software (2022)

46. Van Knippenberg, D., De Dreu, C.K., Homan, A.C.: Work group diversity and group performance: an integrative model and research agenda. J. Appl. Psychol. **89**(6), 1008 (2004)

47. Van Knippenberg, D., Schippers, M.C.: Work group diversity. Annu. Rev. Psychol. **58**, 515–541 (2007)

48. Przybylek, A., Albecka, M., Springer, O., Kowalski, W.: Game-based Sprint retrospectives: multiple action research. Empir Software Eng **27**, 1 (2022). https://doi.org/10.1007/s10664-021-10043-z

49. Kowalczyk, M., Marcinkowski, B., Przybyłek, A.: Scaled agile framework. dealing with software process-related challenges of a financial group with the action research approach. J. Softw. Evol. Process **34**(6), e2455 (2022). https://doi.org/10.1002/smr.2455

50. Joskowski, A., Przybyłek, A., Marcinkowski, B.: Scaling scrum with a customized nexus framework: a report from a joint industry-academia research project. Softw. Pract. Experience **53**(7), 1525–1542 (2023). https://doi.org/10.1002/spe.3201

51. Ahmad, M.O., Dennehy, D., Conboy, K., Oivo, M.: Kanban in software engineering: a systematic mapping study. J. Syst. Softw. **137**, 96–113 (2018). https://doi.org/10.1016/j.jss.2017.11.045

52. Ahmad, M.O., Lwakatare, L.E., Kuvaja, P., Oivo, M., Markkula, J.: An empirical study of portfolio management and Kanban in agile and lean software companies. J. Softw. Evol. Process **29**(6), e1834 (2017). https://doi.org/10.1002/smr.1834

An Association Rule Mining for Selection Requirement Elicitation and Analysis Techniques in IT Projects

Denys Gobov[1] and Nikolay Sokolovskiy[2(✉)]

[1] National Technical University of Ukraine "Igor Sikorsky Kyiv Polytechnic Institute",
37, Prosp. Peremohy, Kyiv, Ukraine
d.gobov@kpi.ua
[2] Independent Researcher, Erevan, Armenia
sokolovskynik@gmail.com

Abstract. Selecting suitable requirements elicitation, specification, and modeling techniques in IT projects is crucial to the business analysis planning process. Typically, the determining factors are the preferences of stakeholders, primarily business analysts, previous experience, and company practices, as well as the availability of sources of information and tools. The influence of other factors is not as evident. One viable method for generating guidance on technique utilization involves the examination of industrial expertise. The primary objective of this research is to investigate the utilization of association rules mining in order to delineate the variables that impact the selection of requirements elicitation and analysis techniques and to forecast the use of specific techniques contingent upon the project's context and the business analyst's profile. Three hundred twenty-eight practitioners from Ukraine's IT industry were surveyed regarding their current practices in business analysis to form a dataset for experiments. The found associations give the potential to expedite the technique selection process in requirement management and enhance the overall efficiency of the business analysis activities.

Keywords: Associations Rules Mining · Requirements Elicitation ·
Requirements Modelling · IT Project · Business Analysis

1 Introduction

All business analysis activities in IT projects can be grouped into six areas: needs assessment, stakeholder management, elicitation, analysis, traceability and monitoring, and solution evaluation [PMI]. While elicitation provides inputs for the core business analysis cycle, specification, and modeling activities provide requirements and designs – the main inputs for further development and testing [2]. The effectiveness of elicitation, specification, and modeling directly depends on the appropriate business analysis approach, which contains decisions regarding who will perform the activities, the timing and sequencing of the work, the deliverables that will be produced, and the that may be utilized [3]. The list of stakeholders, time, and budget constraints are unique for each

A. Jarzębowicz et al. (Eds.): KKIO 2023, LNBIP 499, pp. 82–96, 2024.
https://doi.org/10.1007/978-3-031-51075-5_4

project, while the set of available business analysis techniques is common for all projects. Professional guides and standards recommend many techniques practitioners use in IT projects. Given limitations in both time and budget, business analysts are compelled to refrain from employing all available techniques and instead select such that align most optimally with the unique conditions of the project at hand. The set of elicitation and analysis techniques exerts a substantial impact on the project schedule, development, and testing activities. This study was undertaken to scrutinize the contemporary techniques employed for elicitation, specification, and modeling within IT projects. Its primary aim was to unearth correlations between the project's context, the profiles of specialists involved, and the techniques chosen for requirement elicitation and analysis through the application of Association Rule Mining.

The paper is the extension of a paper [4] originally published in the Proceedings of the Federated Conference on Computer Science and Information Systems 2023. Research findings have been expanded by the result of applying Association Rule Mining for analysis of context influence for requirement specification and modeling techniques and more detailed analysis of dependencies between count of rules, support, and confidence level.

The dataset for examination was formed by surveying 328 IT professionals working for both Ukrainian-based and international companies with local subsidiaries [5]. The strong associations identified with Association Rule Mining made it possible to formulate recommendations on using requirements elicitation, specification, and modeling techniques in IT projects.

2 Problem Statement

The task of selecting best-suited techniques, particularly requirements elicitation and analysis techniques, is performed by a business analyst at the start of the project due to defining and estimating a list of business analysis-related activities. But that does not mean it is a one-time task, and a list of used techniques can be updated based on the efficiency monitoring results and project context changes. Considering that the requirements elicitation and analysis lay the foundation for further development and testing activities, the optimal itechniques selection is an essential business analysis task. The emergence of new techniques and their development in the process of business analysis evolution, as well as the continuously changing business environment, can lead to the complications of this task. A recommendation system that considers the accumulated experience of practicing business analysts and requirements engineers can be applied to solve this problem. An essential condition is the explainability of these recommendations, which will allow for checking their applicability in the unique context of each project.

3 The Best Existing Solution

The problem under study might be divided into several parts: choosing the proper requirement elicitation techniques and choosing the proper analysis techniques.

There are many studies regarding solving the choosing appropriate requirement elicitation technique problem using different approaches and models.

Hatim Dafaalla et al. [6] built a model based on an artificial neuronal network (ANN). The model was learned based on the collected dataset with 1684 records about selecting the elicitation technique. By choosing the ROC AUC metric as a score of the model, the authors achieved significant accuracy of the model, which was equal to 82%. Despite good forecasting by modeling, as with any other ANN, this model has a significant weakness. ANN is a net of perceptron (miniature models of neurons). The perceptron is organized in layers, which are connected. The connections might have a different architecture. Each connection of each perceptron has a weight coefficient. The learning process is a process to optimize these coefficients. Unfortunately, a single coefficient and a set of coefficients don't have meaning and can't be explained in business terms. Similarly, connections, layers, and perceptions do not have any sense separately and don't explain how ANN solved a problem. That is the way some decisions of an ANN might be seen as strange, unexplained, and untrusted [7].

Nagy Ramadan Darwish et al. [8] suggested a hybrid approach. The manuscript describes a pipeline of methods. The feature is manually selected based on literature reviews. Then, a multiple linear regression model was built to select critical attributes influencing technique selection. In the last stage, the ANN was built. The accuracy of the final model was declared as 81%. Despite the remarkable result, the final model has the same limitations as discussed previously. Ihor Bodnarchuk et al. [9] applied goal function for assessment and selection architecture design in the context of "light-weighted" requirements techniques.

Different machine learning approaches were applied not only to technique selection but to related areas as well. Fadhl Hujainah and others [10] suggested using a semi-automated attribute measurement criteria method for requirement prioritization and selection.

A similar method - attributes-based decision making was described by Jinyu Li [11]. Remarkably, semi-automated methods bring a possibility of bias since experts conducted the first assessment.

Considering the modeling techniques as a form of representation and could be separated from the requirements themselves, we discovered few studies addressing how the project context and requirements modeling techniques are connected. Even these works concentrate on relations between particular types of requirements and project context but do not consider requirements and modeling techniques as separate entities. For example, S. Tariq et al. describe relations between non-functional requirements and project context [12]. M. Santos Soares et al. describe relations between user requirements and software-intensive system context [13]. Additionally, all discovered studies use an expert approach and literature review, which allow us to raise the question of what relations could be discovered based on applying machine learning algorithms to survey data collected in the previous paper [14].

4 The Proposed Solution

Associate Rule Mining (ARM) method is a machine-learning technique that combines several remarkable advantages. Firstly, it doesn't require data annotation because it is an unsupervised method. Secondly, the method and output are intuitive and could be understood by domain experts and business people, a rare property of a machine-learning algorithm.

ARM, also known as basket analysis, was applied first in retail, but now it is widely applied in other areas. For example, Giovanna Castro and colleagues in [15] applied association rules to study the comorbidity of bipolar disorder and premenstrual dysphoric disorder. Chad Creighton [16] used association rules to discover hidden gene expression patterns. Ahmad Mirabadi and Shabnam Sharifian [17] applied the ARM to Iranian Railways data to discover patterns leading to incidents and create management manuals and guidelines. Finally, the method could detect credit card fraud [18]. The Association rules are even included in other algorithms, such as Lamma and other [19] embedded AR, as part of the SLA algorithm.

5 Details of the Proposed Solution

5.1 Association Rule Mining

The problem of discovering association rules was proposed by Agrawal et al. [20]. Let $I = \{i_1, i_2, ..., i_m\}$ be a set of m m items. Let T be a set of transaction $\{t_1, t_2, ..., t_n\}$, where each t_i is set of items in which $t_i \subseteq I$. Association rules are implication rules:

$$A \Rightarrow B,$$

which is interpreted as "if A, then B". The following statements must be met: $A \subset I$, $B \subset I$ and $A \cap B = \emptyset$. The A term is an antecedent of the rule. The B term is a consequent of the rule.

The number of rules might be huge, so we need some mechanism for selecting strong rules from weak ones. To do that, let's postulate the following hyperparameters:

- Confidence is a measure that counts how many transactions in T that contain A also contain B. It is the probability of B being true when we already know that A is true:

$$Confidence(A \rightarrow B) = \frac{Occurence\ of\ A\ and\ B}{Occurences\ of\ A} \quad (1)$$

- Support is a measure of the frequency of the transaction patterns that occur in the T:

$$Support(A \Rightarrow B) = \frac{Occurence\ of\ A\ and\ B}{Total\ transaction\ in\ T} \quad (2)$$

- Lift is a value that gives us information about the increase in the probability of the "then" (consequent) given the "if" (antecedent) part. If the lift equals one, we consider there are no dependencies, but if the lift is more than one, we can consider a dependency. Additionally, the lift can demonstrate the "power" of dependency: the larger the lift, the stronger the rule.

$$Lift(A \Rightarrow B) = \frac{Support(A \Rightarrow B)}{Support(A)*Support(B)} \tag{3}$$

So, we can define the minimal support and confidence values to select strong rules. The rules which have confidence more than the selected minimal value are called strong rules.

5.2 Apriori Algorithm

The Apriori, proposed by Agrawal et al. in [20], is an algorithm for discovering association rules. The algorithm is based on searching frequent itemsets. It assumes that if rule X has a confidence level of C and $X \subset Y$, rule Y has a confidence level not less than X. In this way, we can dramatically reduce calculations by excluding many weak rules from consideration based on the frequency of every single i in I.

We used the apriori v1.1.2 python package distributed under MIT license to perform rule mining [21].

5.3 Choosing Hyperparameters

As described above, ARM requires settled initial (apriori) hyperparameters that influence the number of found rules. Usually, these metrics come from the business perspective and domain expert knowledge. Despite some researchers proposing different solutions such as utility functions [22] or prioritization rules technique [23], these and similar approaches could not be applied in the current study because we use the algorithm for discovering new implications and do not have utility function or similar metrics which could be expressed in terms of the value of the particular rule.

However, we still must choose optimal hyperparameters. During the study, we worked with two hyperparameters: support and confidence (see definitions in the next section). According to the study purpose, we are interested in the rules that are big enough to discover insights but small enough for a manual review. The last condition means that when we receive some subset of rules containing more than three items but differentiating only one or two of them, we will likely not discover a significant new implication. Also, we suggested that such rules will have small support and confidence levels (more items - less probability), so we can rely on decreasing the number of rules while increasing minimal support and minimal confidence hyperparameters. In so doing, we can balance the number of rules and the reasonability to find the most appropriate rules among considering combinations.

For choosing hyperparameters, we began with a support level of 0.5, increasing by 0.1 while reaching 1.0. We chose 0.5, which means a rule is true for 50% of cases and allows us to form recommendations for professionals. We obtained an itemset with confidence levels from 0.1 to 1.0 with increments of 0.1 for each new support. Each obtained dataset was estimated among the received rule number to find a vast reduction. Such datasets were reviewed manually, and the uniqueness of contained rules was assessed. We stopped the process when we got a set with completely different rules at the top of the list.

5.3.1 Choosing Hyperparameters for (Project Context ⇒ Elicitation Techniques) Rules

The dependency of rule number on minimal support and minimal confidence values for rules (Project Context ⇒ Elicitation Techniques) is shown in Fig. 1.

The minimal support level has the most influence on rules number. The most significant decrease happened between 0.5 and 0.6 values of the parameter. The minimal confidence does not influence the number of rules in the beginning scale (up to 0.5), influences a bit at 0.6 and 0.7, and only 0.8 value significantly reduces the number of rules. The isolated graphs show the described dynamics (see Fig. 2).

So, we chose the minimal support value equal to 0.5 and the minimal confidence value as 0.8 for mining (Project Context ⇒ Elicitation Techniques) rules.

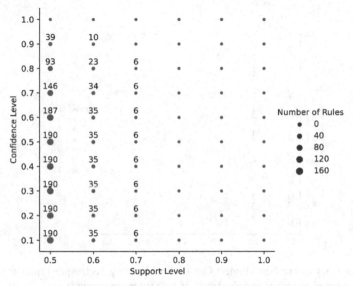

Fig. 1. Dependency of numbers (Project Context ⇒ Elicitation Techniques) rules from minimal support and minimal confidence levels (labels of zero value are omitted)

5.3.2 Choosing Hyperparameters for (Project Context ⇒ Specification and Modelling Techniques) Rules

Consider choosing the hyperparameters for rules (Project Context ⇒ Specification and Modelling Techniques). Building a similar graph of dependency hyperparameter values on the number of the rules (Fig. 3).

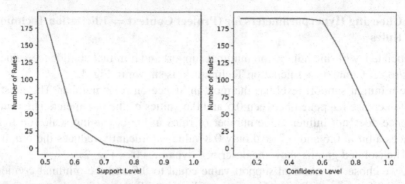

Fig. 2. Dependency of numbers (Project Context ⇒ Elicitation Techniques) rules from minimal support and confidence values separately

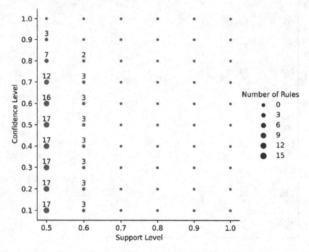

Fig. 3. Dependency of numbers (Project Context ⇒ Modeling Techniques) rules from minimal support and minimal confidence levels (labels of zero value are omitted)

Despite the number of rules with minimal values of hyperparameters being smaller than for (Project Context ⇒ Elicitation Techniques) rules (17 against 190), the behavior of rules dynamics looks the same. The minimal support level value significantly influences the number of rules. 0.6 minimal support cuts almost all rules in the set. The minimal confidence value does not decrease the number of rules until 0.5 value. The gap occurs at 0.7 (from 12 to 7). Isolated graphs of hyperparameter values show the same results (Fig. 4).

For further analysis, we chose minimal support 0.5 and minimal confidence 0.7.

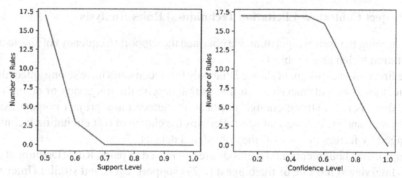

Fig. 4. Dependency of numbers (Project Context ⇒ Modeling Techniques) rules from minimal support and confidence values separately

5.4 Conditions of the Analysis to Follow

Considered methods are applied to the dataset for extraction association rules. It means that if the initial dataset is biased, the found association rules will also have bias.

As described in the above section, choosing hyperparameters includes an expert assessment that could be potentially biased. We organized a cross-review of the obtained results to reduce the potential number of missing rules.

6 Analysis

6.1 Input Data

To discover association rules, we used the survey results conducted in 2020 [24]. After data cleaning, the dataset has 324 answers, which will be treated as a transaction. To describe a project context, we asked respondents about the following:

- project size;
- project domain;
- company type (IT-outstaff, IT-outsource, IT product, non-IT);
- company size;
- class of the developed system (business software, embedded software, scientific, etc.);
- belonging to the co-located or distributed team;
- role in the project;
- years of experience;
- passing certification in the chosen role;
- using adaptive, hybrid, or predictive ways of working on the project;
- project category (developing from scratch, reengineering, product or platform customization, etc.);
- involving in different Types of BA activities.

We ask respondents about their current practices regarding elicitation techniques, requirements specification, and modeling to gather association rules.

Together, the answer's options produced 115 possible items in the itemset.

The dataset is available at the Mendeley Data repository [25].

6.2   (Project Context ⇒ Elicitation Techniques) Rules Analysis

Before running the apriori algorithm, we obtained the support (frequency) of single items of elicitation techniques (Table 1).

The first look at consequent showed that only two techniques have strong antecedents: Document analysis and Interviews. It means that despite the frequency of other consequents, there is not a strong enough implication between any project context aspects under interest and the consequent itself. Perhaps the choice of rest elicitation techniques is managed by factors that lay off the considered dataset.

Remarkably, both mentioned methods are often used in pairs. Rule (Document analysis ⇒ Interviews) has one of the biggest (0.77) support levels and similar (Interviews ⇒ Document analysis). This fact makes sense: a business analyst uses different sources of information due to business analysis information elicitation. Usually, documents and people are the most valuable and accessible sources.

Table 1.   Elicitation techniques with a frequency of more than 0.5.

Elicitation Technique	Support level
Interviews	0.87
Document analysis	0.85
Interface analysis	0.71
Brainstorming	0.69
Process analysis/modeling	0.66
Prototyping	0.66
Business rules analysis	0.54

6.2.1   Document Analysis Association Rules

First, some rules state implications based on other elicitation methods presented in Table 2.

Table 2.   Document analysis association rules

Association Rule	Support level	Confidence level	Lift
Interface analysis ⇒ Document analysis	0.65	0.91	1.06
Process analysis & modeling ⇒ Document analysis	0.6	0.91	1.06
Brainstorming ⇒ Document analysis	0.6	0.87	1.01
Prototyping ⇒ Document analysis	0.58	0.88	1.03

Also, a small subset of rules combines different elicitation methods and another aspect of the project context. For example (here and further, the number in parentheses is a support level): (Business software, Interviews ⇒ Document analysis) (0.69), (Interviews, BA Role ⇒ Document analysis) (0.69), (Business software, Interviews, BA Role ⇒ Document analysis) (0.62), (Interface analysis, Role: BA ⇒ Document analysis) (0.58), (Interface analysis, Interviews ⇒ Document analysis) (0.58). But these rules have support levels smaller than in rules without other components.

Consider other strongest association rules in this group. Remarkably, BA's role in the project implicates using Document analysis: (BA Role ⇒ Document analysis) (0.76), and the rule includes the class of the system under interest: (Business software ⇒ Document analysis) also has a high (0.74) support level. The situation with mixed rules for role and class system is the same as for mixed rules of elicitation techniques: they have more minor support levels and confidence than the short version. For example, (Business software, Role: BA ⇒ Document analysis) (0.67), (Role: BA, Requirements analysis and design definition) (0.58).

For the listed rules, the confidence level is 0.9, and the lift is in the range 1 – 1.09.

Behind the discovered rules, one more group influences the choice of elicitation techniques. The rule with the strongest support level is (Requirements analysis and design definition, Elicitation & Collaboration ⇒ Document analysis) (0.57).

6.2.2 Interviews Association Rules

The Interview's association rules are presented in Table 3.

Table 3. Interview association rules

Association Rule	Support level	Confidence level	Lift
Business software ⇒ Interviews	0.77	0.89	1.02
BA Role ⇒ Interviews	0.76	0.88	1.02
Elicitation & Collaboration ⇒ Interviews	0.63	0.88	1.0
Interface analysis ⇒ Interviews	0.63	0.88	1.01
Brainstorming ⇒ Interviews	0.62	0.91	1.04
Process analysis & modeling ⇒ Interviews	0.60	0.92	1.05
Team distributed ⇒ Interviews	0.55	0.88	1.01

As well as for the previous group, there are many more complex rules with three or more antecedents. However, the support level of these rules is less than the listed above, while their confidence level and lift stay the same. Several examples illustrate the thesis: (Business software, BA Role, Document analysis ⇒ Interviews) (0.62), (Requirements analysis and design definition, Elicitation & Collaboration → Interviews) (0.57), (BA Role, Requirements analysis and design definition ⇒ Interviews) (0.57), (Business software, Requirements analysis and design definition, Elicitation & Collaboration ⇒

Table 4. Modeling techniques with a frequency of more than 0.5

Elicitation Technique	Support level
User Stories	0.78
Use Cases	0.65
Acceptance and Evaluation Criteria	0.63
Sketches/Wireframes	0.54
Activity diagrams	0.53
Business process models	0.52

Interviews) (0.51), (Business software, Document analysis, Process analysis & modeling ⇒ Interviews) (0.5) (Table 4).

That could mean that a significant and essential implication in choosing the elicitation technique is laid out in less complex rules. Remarkable that here we can observe rules that postulate implications based on another elicitation technique, such as Interface analysis and Brainstorming.

6.3   (Project Context⇒Modeling Techniques) Rules Analysis

Launch the algorithm across Modeling Techniques to discover the support level of single modeling techniques with a frequency of more than 0.5:

Analyzing the obtained list, we might notice that User Stories is the only item with a very high support level. Use Case and Acceptance Criteria are in the middle of the list. And all other items have much less support value. The bottom half of the table exceeds the set threshold by a small number (0.02 – 0.04). All found rules are provided in Table 5.

The first obvious conclusion is that User Stories is not only the most frequent item but also the most frequent consequent. Nine of the twelve found associated rules have User Stories in the right part. We noticed that the strongest rules contain tiny related items: User Stories, Acceptance Criteria, and Role: BA. Accordingly, there are several associated rules based on them. And all of them have similar confidence and left values. The rule (Role: BA ⇒ User stories) has a bit higher support level (0.7) than two reciprocal rules: (Acceptance and Evaluation Criteria ⇒ User Stories) and (User Stories ⇒ Acceptance and Evaluation Criteria). Both rules have the same support (0.58) and lift, but (User Stories ⇒ Acceptance and Evaluation Criteria) has less confidence level. Together, it means that a person acting as a Business Analyst usually chooses User Stories as a requirement modeling technique, and they often use Acceptance Criteria as an additional technique. Interestingly, the Acceptance Criteria is used more often with User stories than vice versa.

Besides that, there is an additional branch of rules based on the Business Software item. We have pretty strong (Business software ⇒ User Stories) (0.68) and its derivatives with more minor support levels, but based on the listed items above (for example, Acceptance and Evaluation Criteria, Business software ⇒ User Stories, support 0.51).

Table 5. LA(Project Context⇒Modeling Techniques) Association Rules.

Association Rule	Support level	Confidence level	Lift
Role: BA ⇒ User Stories	0.70	0.81	1.03
Business software ⇒ User Stories	0.68	0.79	1.01
Role: BA, Business software ⇒ User Stories	0.61	0.80	1.02
Acceptance and Evaluation Criteria ⇒ User Stories	0.58	0.92	1.17
User Stories ⇒ Acceptance and Evaluation Criteria	0.58	0.73	1.17
Use Cases ⇒ User Stories	0.54	0.83	1.06
Acceptance and Evaluation Criteria, Role: BA ⇒ User Stories	0.52	0.93	1.18
Role: BA, User Stories ⇒ Acceptance and Evaluation Criteria	0.52	0.75	1.20
Role: BA, Requirements analysis and design definition ⇒ User Stories	0.52	0.79	1.01
Acceptance and Evaluation Criteria, Business software ⇒ User Stories	0.51	0.92	1.18
User Stories, Business software ⇒ Acceptance and Evaluation Criteria	0.51	0.75	1.19
Team distributed ⇒ User Stories	0.50	0.80	1.02

There are only three isolated associated rules, which are based on other items (in order of support decreasing):

- Use Case
- Requirements analysis and design definition
- Team distributed.

All rules based on these items have User Stories in consequents. All of them have very strong confidence (0.79–0.83) but small lift (1.01–1.06).

7 Conclusion

We analyzed datasets obtained from the survey regarding current practices in requirement elicitation, specification, and modeling in IT projects conducted in Ukraine. The dataset includes 324 transactions containing items from the 115 items. The apriori algorithm was used for discovering association rules. The algorithm discovered 86 (Project Context ⇒ Elicitations Techniques) and 12 (Project Context ⇒ Modeling Techniques) associated rules. Parameters for found rules were analyzed.

The most frequently used elicitation techniques are Interviews, Document analysis, Brainstorming, Process analysis and modeling, Prototyping, and Business rules analysis. The main discovering facts about elicitation techniques rules are:

- Among all frequent rules, only two techniques - Document analysis and Interviews-form strong association rules with project context.
- Interviews and Document analysis are used together pretty often.
- Class of developing system (business software) and BA role and BA activity increase the likelihood of using Document Analysis as an elicitation technique.
- Class of developing system (business software) and BA role, distributed team, Process analysis & modeling, and BA activity such as Elicitation and Collaboration increase the likelihood of using of Interview technique.
- Some elicitation techniques (Brainstorming, Interface analysis, Process analysis & modeling) entail the use of the Interview technique.
- The combination class of developing system, role in the project, team distribution, and activity with other aspects of project context have more minor support levels than less complex rules having only one antecedent and could be considered a sub-option.

User Stories, Use Cases and Acceptance and Evaluation Criteria are the most frequently used requirements specification and modeling techniques.

The following recommendations can be proposed based on found association rules:

- If a person is a Business Analyst, they should consider User Stories as a basic form of requirements modeling techniques
- User Stories and Acceptance and Evaluation Criteria should be used together
- User Stories are also suitable for Requirements analysis and design definition
- User Stories might complete Use Cases
- Class of developing system (business software), distributed team involve the use of User Stories as well.

Further research can be conducted to explore the results of other surveys conducted with practitioners involved from different countries to check the recommendations defined in this study, as well as extend the set of rules by using additional project context attributes and business analysis elements.

References

1. Pohl, K.: Requirements engineering: fundamentals, principles, and techniques. Springer, New York, USA (2010)
2. Gobov, D., Yanchuk, V.: Network analysis application to analyze the activities and artifacts in the core business analysis cycle. In: 2021 2nd International Informatics and Software Engineering Conference (IISEC), pp. 1–6. IEEE, Ankara, Turkey (2021). https://doi.org/10.1109/IISEC54230.2021.9672373
3. International Institute of Business Analysis: A guide to the business analysis body of knowledge (BABOK Guide). 3rd ed. International Institute of Business Analysis, Toronto, Ontario, Canada (2015)

4. Gobov, D., Sokolovskiy, N.: Association rule mining for requirement elicitation techniques in IT projects. In: 18th Federated Conference on Computer Science and Information Systems, ACSIS, vol. 35, pp. 983–987 (2023). https://doi.org/10.15439/2023F4831
5. Gobov, D.: Practical study on software requirements specification and modelling techniques. Int. J. Comput. **22**(1), 78–86 (2023). https://doi.org/10.47839/ijc.22.1.2882
6. Dafaalla, H., et al.: Deep learning model for selecting suitable requirements elicitation techniques. Appl. Sci. **12**(18), 9060 (2022). https://doi.org/10.3390/app12189060
7. Sharma, V., Rai, S., Dev, A.: A comprehensive study of artificial neural networks. Int. J. Adv. Res. Comput. Sci. Softw. Eng. **2**(10), 278–284 (2012)
8. Darwish, N., Mohamed, A., Abdelghany, A.: A hybrid machine learning model for selecting suitable requirements elicitation techniques. Int. J. Comput. Sci. Inf. Secur. **14**(6), 1–12 (2016)
9. Bodnarchuk, I., et al.: Adaptive method for assessment and selection of software architecture in flexible techniques of design. In: 13th International Scientific and Technical Conference on Computer Sciences and Information Technologies (CSIT), pp. 292–297. IEEE, Lviv, Ukraine (2018). https://doi.org/10.1109/stc-csit.2018.8526620
10. Hujainah, F., Bakar, R.B.A., Abdulgabber, M.A.: StakeQP: A semi-automated stakeholder quantification and prioritization technique for requirement selection in software system projects. Decis. Support. Syst. **121**, 94–108 (2019). https://doi.org/10.1016/j.dss.2019.04.009
11. Li, J., et al.: Attributes-based decision making for selection of requirement elicitation techniques using the analytic network process. Math. Probl. Eng. **2020**, 1–13 (2020). https://doi.org/10.1155/2020/2156023
12. Tariq S., Cheema, S. M.: Approaches for non-functional requirement modeling: a literature survey. In 4th International Conference on Computing & Information Sciences (ICCIS), pp. 1–6. IEEE, Karachi, Pakistan (2021). https://doi.org/10.1109/ICCIS54243.2021.9676398
13. Soares, M.S., Vrancken, J., Verbraeck, A.: User requirements modeling and analysis of software-intensive systems. J. Syst. Softw. **84**(2), 328–339 (2011)
14. Gobov, D., Huchenko, I.: Modern requirements documentation techniques and the influence of the project context: Ukrainian it experience. In: Hu, Z., Dychka, I., Petoukhov, S., He, M. (eds.) Advances in Computer Science for Engineering and Education. ICCSEEA 2022. Lecture Notes on Data Engineering and Communications Technologies, vol. 134. Springer, Cham (2022). https://doi.org/10.1007/978-3-031-04812-8_22
15. Castro, G., et al.: Applying association rules to study bipolar disorder and premenstrual dysphoric disorder comorbidity. In: 2018 IEEE Canadian Conference on Electrical & Computer Engineering (CCECE), pp. 1–4. IEEE, Quebec, QC, Canada (2018). https://doi.org/10.1109/ccece.2018.8447747
16. Creighton, C., Hanash, S.: Mining gene expression databases for association rules. Bioinformatics **19**(1), 79–86 (2003). https://doi.org/10.1093/bioinformatics/19.1.79
17. Mirabad, A., Sharifian, S.: Application of association rules in Iranian Railways (RAI) accident data analysis. Saf. Sci. **48**(10), 1427–1435 (2010). https://doi.org/10.1016/j.ssci.2010.06.006
18. Sánchez, D., et al.: Association rules applied to credit card fraud detection. Expert Syst. Appl. **36**(2), 3630–3640 (2009). https://doi.org/10.1016/j.eswa.2008.02.001
19. Lamma, E., et al.: Improving the SLA algorithm using association rules. In: Cappelli, A., Turini, F. (eds.) AI*IA 2003: Advances in Artificial Intelligence. AI*IA 2003. LNCS, vol. 2829. Springer, Berlin, Heidelberg (2003). https://doi.org/10.1007/978-3-540-39853-0_14
20. Agrawal, R., et al.: Fast algorithms for mining association rules. In: 20th International Conference Very Large Data Bases, pp. 487–499. Morgan Kaufmann Publishers Inc., San Francisco, CA, USA (1994)
21. Github. https://github.com/ymoch/apyori. Accessed 22 Oct 2023
22. Hikmawati, E., Maulidevi, N.U., Surendro, K.: Minimum threshold determination method based on dataset characteristics in association rule mining. J. Big Data **8**, 1–17 (2021)

23. Choi, D.H., Ahn, B.S., Kim, S.H.: Prioritization of association rules in data mining: multiple criteria decision approach. Expert Syst. Appl. **29**(4), 867–878 (2005). https://doi.org/10.1016/j.eswa.2005.06.006
24. Gobov, D., Huchenko, I.: Influence of the software development project context on the requirements elicitation techniques selection. In: Hu, Z., Petoukhov, S., Dychka, I., He, M. (eds.) Advances in Computer Science for Engineering and Education IV. ICCSEEA 2021. Lecture Notes on Data Engineering and Communications Technologies, vol. 83. Springer, Cham (2021). https://doi.org/10.1007/978-3-030-80472-5_18
25. Mendeley Data. https://data.mendeley.com/datasets/svzv7rs279. Accessed 22 Oct 2023

Track on Software, System and Service Engineering (S3E 2023)

Exploring Relationships Between Data in Enterprise Information Systems by Analysis of Log Contents

Łukasz Korzeniowski[1]([✉]) [ID] and Krzysztof Goczyła[2] [ID]

[1] Nordea Bank Abp SA, Satamaradankatu 5, 00020 Helsinki, Finland
lukasz.korzeniowski@protonmail.com
[2] Gdańsk University of Technology, Faculty of Electronics,
Telecommunication and Informatics, Narutowicza 11/12, Gdańsk, Poland
kris@eti.pg.edu.pl

Abstract. Enterprise systems are inherently complex and maintaining their full, up-to-date overview poses a serious challenge to the enterprise architects' teams. This problem encourages the search for automated means of discovering knowledge about such systems. An important aspect of this knowledge is understanding the data that are processed by applications and their relationships. In our previous work, we used application logs of an enterprise system to derive knowledge about the interactions taking place between applications. In this paper, we further explore logs to discover correspondence between data processed by different applications. Our contribution is the following: we propose a method for discovering relationships between data using log analysis, we validate our method against a real-life system running at Nordea Bank, we provide detailed insights into a real-life dataset, we analyze the influence of log quality on the results provided by our method, and we provide recommendations for developers on logging practices that can support the log analysis.

Keywords: Log analysis · Enterprise systems · Data mining · Reverse engineering · Unsupervised learning

1 Introduction

Large enterprises, especially those with a long history of operation, face the challenge of modernizing their processes and adapting them to the changing environment. One of the key, and often the most challenging, aspects of such adaptation is the modernization of the enterprise's IT infrastructure. This is usually a complex endeavor, that includes exiting legacy systems, reorganizing the architecture, and harmonizing the data usage across the enterprise system. Each of these activities requires the enterprise architects team to have a good

Supported by the Gdańsk University of Technology and Nordea Bank.

understanding of the existing IT infrastructure constituting the enterprise system, including the processes, applications participating in them, and the data being processed.

In [8] we proposed a method for discovering the knowledge about the interactions between applications in an enterprise system based on the analysis of application logs. We chose this type of analysis as the basis for our method due to some interesting properties of logs. Firstly, logging is a common practice present in IT from its very beginning, meaning that both legacy and modern applications are expected to create some sort of log (a trace of the actions executed by an application). Secondly, logs contain rich information, which blends the working application's technical and business aspects. Lastly, log entries tend to be kept up-to-date with the executed application code. All of these properties make application logs a perfect candidate for deriving the actual knowledge about various aspects of the enterprise system in an automated way.

In [9], we explored the potential of application log analysis in terms of supplying enterprise architects with valuable information about the enterprise system. We focused on the data processed by applications. We tried to find correspondence between data processed by different applications, which can be treated as good candidates for reconstructing relationships between data models used by different applications of the system. This information can be valuable in many aspects - it allows for the "detection" of pieces of information used by various applications, it allows for explaining information from legacy applications by finding its correspondence to information in modern (well-documented) applications, and it allows for attaching some business meaning to information by utilizing the business part of log entries. We validated the proposed method on two datasets: open-source based on AcmeAir application [2] and NDEASET2 based on a real-life system running at Nordea Bank, however detailed results were provided only for the open-source dataset.

This paper extends [9] by providing detailed results of the application of our method on a real-life dataset from Nordea Bank. Additionally, we analyze the influence of the log quality on the outcome of our method. We provide recommendations for developers' logging practices that would support reaching the best results by our algorithm. We also extend our method by introducing an additional strategy for token embedding.

The rest of the paper is organized as follows. In Sect. 2, we present a formal statement of the problem. Section 3 describes the proposed method of log analysis. In Sect. 4, we introduce the dataset used for the evaluation of our method, define the evaluation criteria, and present the results. In Sect. 5, we compare our method with alternative approaches and describe the related work. We present the conclusions and plans for future work in Sect. 6.

2   Problem Statement

Let enterprise system S consists of a set of applications $A = \{a_1, \ldots, a_n\}$. Let each application $a_i \in A$ process some data represented by a set of data attributes

a1: Client management		a2: Account management		a3: Cash Transfers	
	socialSecurityNumber		IBAN		sourceAccount
	name		accountOwner		targetAccount
D1	surname	D2	accCurrency	D3	transferCurrency
	address		balance		amount
	email				

Fig. 1. An example of a fragment of an enterprise system S from the banking domain, related to the execution of cash transfers. The yellow color denotes different applications constituting the system. Red, green, and blue colors denote the data attributes processed by each of the applications. (Color figure online)

$D^i = \{d_1^i, \ldots, d_{k^i}^i\}$. For each data attribute $d_k^i \in D^i$, we denote the set of potential values that the attribute can take by $V(i, k)$.

A fragment of an example enterprise system with applications and respective data attributes is presented in Fig. 1. The presented fragment is related to the processing of cash transfers in a bank and consists of three applications - managing clients, managing accounts, and cash transfer execution.

For any two data attributes d_k^i, d_l^j, we define their level of similarity using the Jaccard index

$$J(d_k^i, d_l^j) = \frac{|V(i, k) \cap V(j, l)|}{|V(i, k) \cup V(j, l)|} \tag{1}$$

We define a data relationship graph $G(S) = (U, E)$ as an undirected graph, where E is the set of edges consisting of all pairs of related data attributes d_k^i, d_l^j, and U is the respective set of vertices. An example of such a graph is presented in Fig. 2.

Let $L(a_i) = (l_1^i, \ldots, l_{k^i}^i)$ denote the log of application $a_i \in A$, represented by a tuple of log entries.

We define the problem of discovering data relationships as follows. Having a set of application logs $L = \{L(a_1), \ldots, L(a_n)\}$, find approximate graph $G' = (U', E')$.

3 Proposed Method

3.1 Method Overview

We propose a method that treats a log as a text. Such an approach has several benefits. It does not require any arbitrary assumptions to be made about the log contents, which results in a broader scope of the method's usability. It also does not require additional preprocessing of the log, apart from unifying the log format across applications. Our method does not require any knowledge of the underlying data attributes for each application - they are discovered from the

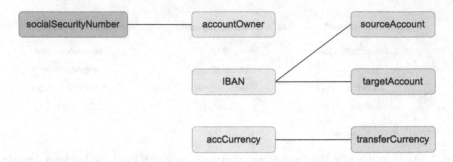

Fig. 2. A data relationship graph for the example system presented in Fig. 1. Edges represent relationships between data attributes from different applications. The coloring of nodes matches the coloring in Fig. 1.

Fig. 3. Overview of data relationship discovery method.

log automatically. Figure 3 presents an overview of the steps that our method consists of.

Our method is parameterized by the following hyper-parameters:

- N - the maximum length of n-gram embedding of a token,
- ies - inner embedding similarity threshold,
- oes - outer embedding similarity threshold,
- mt - minimum number of tokens sharing the same embedding that is required for the embedding to be considered,
- ml - minimum length for a token to be considered valid.

The following subsections describe each of the steps in detail. For better understanding, we provide a set of figures forming a running example. The example is based on the open-source AcmeAir application [2].

3.2   Token Embedding

We process the log of each application $a \in A$ separately. For each log entry, we extract a list of tokens using the regular expression $[@.A - Za - z0 - 9_-]+$. For each token in the log entry and each $k \in \{1, \ldots, N\}$, we create its embedding as a k-gram of words [11]. We use two alternative embedding strategies, which we further evaluate in Sect. 4:

- simple - we take k tokens preceding the given token in the log line,
- hierarchical - for log lines representing a hierarchical content that can be represented as a tree (e.g. XML or SWIFT messages), we take a path of k nodes from the node representing the given token, towards the tree's root. For other types of log lines, we use the simple strategy.

```
122342134,D,Received message:        122342134,D,Received message:
<?xml version="1.0" ?>               <?xml version="1.0" ?>
<CdtTrfTxInf>                        <CdtTrfTxInf>
   <IntrBkSttlmAmt                      <IntrBkSttlmAmt
Ccy='USD'>12500</IntrBkSttlmAmt>     Ccy='USD'>12500</IntrBkSttlmAmt>
   <IntrBkSttlmDt>2019-10-              <IntrBkSttlmDt>2019-10-
29</IntrBkSttlmDt>                   29</IntrBkSttlmDt>
   <Dbtr>                               <Dbtr>
      <Nm>ACME NV.</Nm>                    <Nm>ACME NV.</Nm>
      <PstlAdr>                            <PstlAdr>
         <StrtNm>Amstel</StrtNm>              <StrtNm>Amstel</StrtNm>
         <BldgNb>344</BldgNb>                 <BldgNb>344</BldgNb>
         <TwnNm>Amsterdam</TwnNm>             <TwnNm>Amsterdam</TwnNm>
         <Ctry>NL</Ctry>                      <Ctry>NL</Ctry>
      </PstlAdr>                            </PstlAdr>
   </Dbtr>                               </Dbtr>
</CdtTrfTxInf>                        </CdtTrfTxInf>
```

Fig. 4. Comparison of the embedding strategies used for encoding the token marked in yellow. Tokens marked in green form its 3-gram embeddings. The left side of the picture presents the embeddings created according to the simple strategy and the right side - embeddings for the hierarchical strategy.

The first strategy is general purpose and can be applied to any type of log message. The latter strategy is expected to result in more accurate embeddings in real-life scenarios, where the same token has different semantics, depending on the context (e.g. XML tags with the same name but different placement in the XML tree). Figure 4 presents an example of embedding the same token according to both strategies.

The k-gram embedding approach means that the same token can have multiple embeddings for a given value of k, depending on the context (consisting of k preceding tokens). An example of such embeddings is presented in Fig. 5. It can be noticed that "NRT", "destPort" and "miles" tokens have different embeddings for both log lines due to different neighbor tokens in each of the lines.

For each value of k and for each unique embedding e, we maintain the set of all tokens sharing this embedding within the $L(a)$, which we denote as $Emb^a(e, k)$. We denote the set of all k-gram embeddings within a as Emb_k^a, and the set of all embeddings within $L(a)$ as $Emb^a = \bigcup_{k \in \{1, \ldots, N\}} Emb_k^a$. Figure 6 shows groups of tokens sharing the same embedding.

For given k-gram embedding e consisting of tokens $(t_k, t_{k-1}, \ldots, t_1)$ and $l < k$, we define an l-cut operation on e, denoted as $e|l$, as follows: $e|l = (t_l, t_{l-1}, \ldots, t_1)$.

3.3   Embedding Optimization

The result of the previous step is ambiguous - the same groups of tokens are represented with multiple embeddings, for different values of $k \in \{1, \ldots, N\}$. To remove this ambiguity, we search for the highest value of k such that k-gram embedding of the groups of tokens represents them better than $k + 1$-gram embedding. The longer the embedding, the more precisely it describes the represented tokens.

Log entries of application a

Line 1: flightsegment = {"_id":"AA382","originPort":"NRT","destPort":"DEL","miles":"4959"}
Line 2: flightsegment = {"_id":"AA87","originPort":"FRA","destPort":„NRT","miles":"400"}

Embeddings for Line 1

Token	1-gram	2-gram
flightsegment		
_id	flightsegment	
AA382	_id	flightsegment, _id
originPort	AA382	_id, AA382
NRT	originPort	AA382, originPort
destPort	NRT	originPort, NRT
DEL	destPort	NRT, destPort
miles	DEL	destPort, DEL
4959	miles	DEL, miles

Embeddings for Line 2

Token	1-gram	2-gram
flightsegment		
_id	flightsegment	
AA87	_id	flightsegment, _id
originPort	AA87	_id, AA87
FRA	originPort	AA87, originPort
destPort	FRA	originPort, FRA
NRT	destPort	FRA, destPort
miles	NRT	destPort, NRT
400	miles	NRT, miles

Fig. 5. 1- and 2-gram simple embeddings for sample log entries. Yellow color denotes tokens with multiple embeddings.

1-gram embeddings

Embedding e	$Emb^a(e,1)$	
flightsegment	_id	
_id	AA382	AA87
AA382	originPort	
originPort	NRT	FRA
NRT	destPort	miles
destPort	DEL	NRT
DEL	miles	
miles	4959	400
AA87	originPort	
FRA	destPort	

2-gram embeddings

Embedding e	$Emb^a(e,2)$	
flightsegment, _id	AA382	AA87
_id, AA382	originPort	
AA382, originPort	NRT	
originPort, NRT	destPort	
NRT, destPort	DEL	
destPort, DEL	miles	
DEL, miles	4959	
_id, AA87	originPort	
AA87, originPort	FRA	
originPort, FRA	destPort	
FRA, destPort	NRT	
destPort, NRT	miles	
NRT, miles	400	

Fig. 6. Tokens sharing the same 1- and 2-gram embedding for sample log entries from Fig. 2.

We start with the set of initial embeddings E that consists of all 1-gram embeddings. For each 2-gram embedding e, we then take the set of all tokens that it represents $Emb^a(e,2)$. We compare this set with the set of all tokens represented as 1-cut of e, using the Jaccard index. If the index value is above the *ies* threshold, we substitute the $e|1$ embedding in E with e. We repeat this procedure for longer k-grams until $k = N$, each time comparing the k-gram embedding with its $k-1$-cut. In the end, the set E contains all the embeddings

k = 1

Initial embeddings

flightsegment	_id	AA382	originPort	NRT
destPort	DEL	Miles	AA87	FRA

k = 2

Embedding e	$Emb^a(e, 2)$		Embedding e	1	$OEmb^a(e|1)$		Jaccard index
flightsegment, _id	AA382	AA87	_id		AA382	AA87	1
_id, AA382	originPort		AA382		originPort		1
AA382, originPort	NRT		originPort		NRT	FRA	0.5
originPort, NRT	destPort		NRT		destPort	miles	0.5
NRT, destPort	DEL		destPort		DEL	NRT	0.5
destPort, DEL	miles		DEL		miles		1
DEL, miles	4959		miles		4959	400	0.5
_id, AA87	originPort		A87		originPort		1
AA87, originPort	FRA		originPort		NRT	FRA	0.5
originPort, FRA	destPort		FRA		destPort		1
FRA, destPort	NRT		destPort		DEL	NRT	0.5
destPort, NRT	miles		NRT		destPort	miles	0.5
NRT, miles	400		miles		4959	400	0.5

Fig. 7. Steps of the example optimization process for embeddings presented in Fig. 6 and *ies* threshold of 0.9. The yellow color denotes the $k - 1$ cut of the embedding. Each row in the table presents a step in the process. Green cells denote the embeddings that have been accepted and red cells denote the embeddings that have been rejected.

for log $L(a)$ after optimization, which we denote as $OEmb^a$. Figure 7 shows the two consecutive steps of the optimization process.

$OEmb^a(e)$ denotes the set of tokens represented by embedding e within log $L(a)$. The above algorithm ensures that there is only one embedding (one value of k) that represents a given set of tokens. Figure 8 presents the example outcome of the optimization process.

3.4 Token Filtering

We further optimize the set of embeddings. For each application log $L(a)$ and each embedding $e \in OEmb^a$:

- we discard e if $|OEmb^a(e)| < mt$,
- we define the filtered set of tokens, such that $\forall_{e \in OEmb} FEmb^a(e) = \{t \in OEmb^a(e) | length(t) \geq ml\}$.

$FEmb^a(e)$ denotes the final set of tokens represented by the embedding e within application log $L(a)$, while $FEmb^a$ represents the set of all final embeddings for application a, and $FEmb = \bigcup_{a \in A} FEmb^a$ is a set of all embeddings in the system.

Initial embedding	Optimized embedding	$OEmb^a$	
flightsegment	flightsegment	_id	
_id	flightsegment, _id	AA382	AA87
AA382	_id, AA382	originPort	
originPort	originPort	NRT	FRA
NRT	NRT	destPort	miles
destPort	destPort	DEL	NRT
DEL	destPort, DEL	miles	
miles	miles	4959	400
AA87	_id, AA87	originPort	
FRA	originPort, FRA	destPort	

Fig. 8. The outcome of the example process presented in Fig. 7 Green cells denote the embeddings that have been extended as part of the optimization.

The first optimization removes embeddings that represent only a few tokens. Such embeddings are interpreted as representations of static parts of the log entry, which are of less interest in terms of data relationship discovery. The second optimization removes short tokens, which decreases the chance of discovering accidental relationships.

3.5   Graph Estimate Construction

We calculate a distance matrix between all $FEmb$ embeddings using the Jaccard index as the distance measure:

$$\forall_{e_1,e_2 \in FEmb, e_1 \neq e_2} dist(e_1, e_2) = \frac{|FEmb(e_1) \cap FEmb(e_2)|}{|FEmb(e_1) \cup FEmb(e_2)|} \qquad (2)$$

We filter pairs of embeddings based on their distance, using oes as the threshold, above which the embedding relationship is considered strong enough and should be retained. The retained embedding pairs form the edges of our approximate graph G' and respective embeddings become the vertices of the graph. Figure 10 presents an example distance matrix for the final embeddings presented in Fig. 9. The respective graph estimate is shown in Fig. 11, which shows a detected relationship between $originPort$ and $destPort$ data attributes.

Final embedding	$FEmb^a$	
flightsegment, _id	AA382	AA87
originPort	NRT	FRA
NRT	destPort	miles
destPort	DEL	NRT
miles	4959	400

Fig. 9. The final set of embeddings for sample log entries presented in Fig. 5.

Distance	flightsegment, _id	originPort	NRT	destPort	miles
flightsegment, _id		0	0	0	0
originPort	0		0	0.33	0
NRT	0	0		0	0
destPort	0	0.33	0		0
miles	0	0	0	0	

Fig. 10. Distance matrix for final embeddings from Fig. 9, based on the Jaccard index.

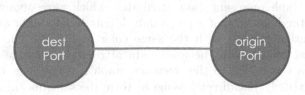

Fig. 11. Graph estimate for the set of final embeddings and *oes* threshold of 0.25.

4 Method Evaluation

4.1 Dataset Overview

We evaluate our method using the NDEASET2 - a dataset from a real-life enterprise system running at Nordea Bank, which we refer to as NDEASYS. As compared to the NDEASET1 dataset described in our previous work [8], NDEASET2 covers a full working week of the NDEASYS. The total size of the dataset is larger by an order of magnitude (95GB). It covers one more application and one additional process (daily reporting). We followed the same rules for removing bias as described in [8] to ensure proper diversity of the dataset, which include:

– team diversity - applications built by teams of different sizes, experiences, locations,

- application diversity - we included dedicated business applications, purely
  technical components, and shared service platforms (e.g., storage or communication services),
- time diversity - applications built in different periods,
- integration diversity - applications communicating using different interfaces
  and exchange formats.

The bias of the dataset related to logs being collected within the same company
is mitigated by the fact that Nordea does not enforce any strict rules for log
creation and log contents for non-regulatory logging.

The fragment of the architecture of the NDEASYS that contributes to the
creation of logs within NDEASET2 is shown in Fig. 12. Applications B and D
are both providing data of the same type to A, but using different formats.
Application A enriches the received data with data from applications C, E, and
F. The final result is aggregated as part of the daily reporting and the aggregated
data are provided to application G.

Table 1 describes the characteristics of the NDEASYS2 dataset. As part of
the log preprocessing, we unify all of the logs in the dataset to a common CSV
format with timestamp, source, and message columns. Figure 13 presents an
anonymized example of log entries in NDEASET2.

Reference Graph. For the sake of further evaluation, we created a reference
graph based on NDEASYS documentation and presented in Fig. 14. Nodes in
the reference graph represent data attributes, which were anonymized. Node
colors denote the belonging of a given data attribute to a data asset managed
by the application marked with the same color in Fig. 12. The edges of the
graph represent relationships between data attributes. An edge between two
data attributes was added to the reference graph if a fragment of NDEASYS
specification existed, that directly assigned them the same meaning.

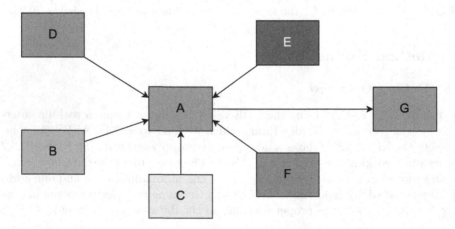

Fig. 12. The architecture of the system used for evaluation. Lines denote pairs of
interacting applications, and arrows denote the direction of the data flow.

Table 1. Characteristics of the NDEASYS2 Dataset

App	Log size [MB]	Application diversity	Team diversity		Time diversity		Integration diversity	
		Type	Size	No. loc.	Dev. period	Dev. duration [months]	Integration style	Format
A	26000	dedicated	3	2	2020-2022	24	Messaging, RPI	Swift (ISO15022, ISO 20022), JSON
B	165	technical	1	2	2020	1	Messaging	Swift (ISO15022)
C	7000	shared service	2	2	2016-2020	48	RPI	JSON
D	18	technical	1	2	2020	6	Messaging	Swift (ISO15022)
E	64000	shared service	3	2	2016-2020	72	RPI	JSON
F	153	shared service	3	2	2016-2020	72	RPI	JSON
G	80	technical	1	2	2020	1	Messaging	Swift (ISO15022

It can be observed that the reference graph is a multi-component graph. Each of the clusters represents a mutual relationship between data attributes. The fact that individual clusters do not form cliques results from the direct mapping of NDEASYS specification to the graph's edges. The specification of each application is usually expressed only in the context of its neighbor applications. Figure 15 presents the histogram of different component sizes. Table 2 shows the number of relationships between data attributes managed by different applications. The intensity of the color reflects the number of relationships.

```
1647330650034,E,"
logger=c.n.t.i.r.q.QueryCallStatsObserver,
operation=QUERY_LATEST_IN_GROUP, clientId=X,
clientLibrary=null, clientVersion=null,
hostName=a01.com, correlationId=969a81d3-8ad8-4a5f-
84e8- 0868bfd65ddb, action=query_start, , domain=Y/Z,
requestCondition={""extracted.id"":
""0122318714085000""},  condition={""extracted.id"":
""0122318714085000""},
groupByFields=[Id], sortFields=[timestamp], limit=0,
payload=true"
```

Fig. 13. Example of one log entry from NDEASET2. Yellow color denotes the timestamp, green - the source application, and cyan - the message.

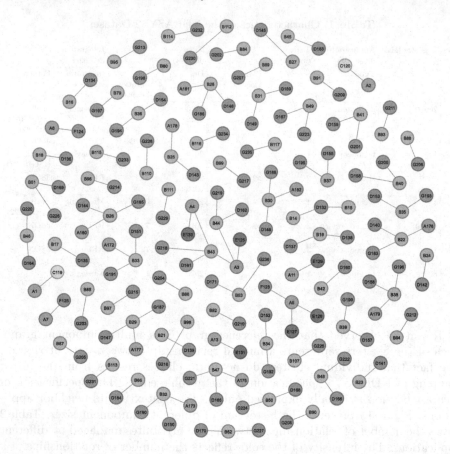

Fig. 14. Reference graph of dependencies between data attributes in NDEASYS. Node colors match the application colors in Fig. 12. All graph visualizations in this Section were created using the Gephi - a graph visualization tool [1].

Log Contents. We analyzed the content of logs constituting the NDEASET2 and categorized each of the log messages (log lines) using two perspectives: the purpose of the message and its content. For classifying the purpose of the log message, we used the following categories:

- Business - log entries related to tracking the business process performed by an application,
- Technical - log entries capturing the inner workings of the underlying technology used by an application.

The content of the log message is categorized into the following classes:

- Access - technical log entry capturing access attempts to the application and accept/reject decisions,
- Action execution - log entry capturing the fact of execution of a business action of an application,

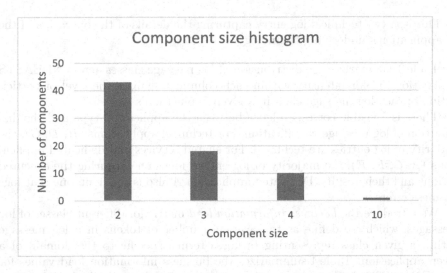

Fig. 15. Histogram of component sizes in the reference graph for NDEASET2 dataset.

Table 2. Breakdown of data attribute relationships to applications.

	A	B	C	D	E	F	G	Total
A	0	13	2	0	6	3	0	24
B	13	0	0	40	0	0	54	107
C	2	0	0	0	0	0	0	2
D	0	40	0	0	0	0	0	40
E	6	0	0	0	0	0	0	6
F	3	0	0	0	0	0	0	3
G	0	54	0	0	0	0	0	54
Total	24	107	2	40	6	3	54	236

- Action result - log entry capturing the result of a business action,
- Action summary - log entry stating the finalization of a business action, without listing its results,
- Decision - log entry notifying the decision path taken by an application while executing business logic,
- Error - log entry notifying about a business error that occurred during application logic execution,
- Event - log entry capturing the fact and details (optionally) of a business event that occurred in an application,
- Performance metrics - technical log entry capturing metrics for the purpose of performance assessment,

- Third-party - technical log entry capturing the details of the operation of the application's underlying technology.

Table 3 summarizes the distribution of log message classes across NDEASYS applications. Color intensity within each column visualizes the level of participation of each log message class in a given application's log.

There is a visible correspondence between the application type and the distribution of log message classification. For technical applications (B, D, G), the majority of log entries are technical. For shared services and dedicated applications (A, C, E, F), the majority of log entries focus on capturing the executed actions and their results. Dedicated application A also is the main one that logs business errors.

We introduce the *business information load* metric for different classes of log messages, which we define as the average number of tokens in a log message within a given class representing business terms, specific to the domain of a given application. Table 4 summarizes the business information load values for the NDEASET2 dataset. Applications B, G, and D have the highest business information load driven mostly by the *event* log message class. These events are entries that log the input received by an application, which is rare compared to the technical log entries in these applications but bears a significant level of business information. A, which is a dedicated application with a substantial amount of business logic, creates more log entries related to the business process, but with fewer details. Shared services, C, E, and F, tend to include only a very minimal level of business details in their logs.

Table 3. Distribution of log message classification across applications in NDEASYS (values given in percentage within an application, rounded to integer numbers).

Purpose	Content	A	B	C	D	E	F	G
Business	Action execution	67	0	42	1	40	49	0
Business	Action result	15	0	41	0	0	47	0
Business	Action summary	0	0	0	0	40	1	0
Business	Decision	0	0	0	8	0	0	0
Business	Error	18	0	0	5	0	0	0
Business	Event	0	0	0	20	20	0	0
Technical	Access	0	0	0	0	0	0	0
Technical	Performance	0	0	17	0	0	4	0
Technical	Third-party	0	100	0	65	1	0	100

Table 4. Average business information load per log message class for NDEASYS applications. Empty cells denote log message classes not available in a given application's log. Color intensity visualizes the relative information load level across the whole dataset.

Log message class	A	B	C	D	E	F	G	Avg
Action execution	4.5		1	0	1.5	1		1.6
Action result	6.4		0			0		2.1
Action summary	0.3			0	0			0.1
Decision	5			1.5		0		2.2
Error	2			1.8	0.6			1.5
Event	1.8	59		29	0		59	29.8
Access					2			2
Performance			0		0	0		0
Third-party	0	0		0	0	0	0	0
Avg	2.8	29.5	0.3	6.5	0.6	0.2	29.5	

4.2 Evaluation Criteria

To evaluate the quality of our method, we use two metrics:

- component accuracy,
- component completeness.

The main reason for using two measures is the fact that the reference graph does not contain all the edges. It is constructed to reflect the system's specification. Each component of the reference graph represents a separate group of related data attributes and could, as such, be expressed as a clique. Using a single metric based on the comparison of the edge sets between the discovered and reference graphs would result in a large number of false negatives due to the construction of the reference graph. The *component accuracy* measure addresses the question of how effective the method was in finding the relationship groups (components) while the *component completeness* measure looks into the internal structure of the discovered components and addresses the question of how well it represents the components of the reference graph.

Component Accuracy. This measure represents how many components from the reference graph we discovered. Let G^R be the reference graph and G^D be the discovered graph. Let $C^R = \bigcup_{i=\{1...n\}} C_i^R$ be the set of all the components of the reference graph, where $C_i^R = (V_i^R, E_i^R)$ is a graph representing the i-th component. Let $C^D = \bigcup_{j=\{1...m\}} C_m^D$ be the set of all the components of the discovered graph, where $C_m^D = (V_j^D, E_j^D)$ is a graph representing the j-th component.

We say that a discovered component $C_k^D = (V_k^D, E_k^D)$ is a true positive if $\exists_{l \in \{1...n\}} E_k \cap E_l \neq \emptyset$. Let TP be the set of all true positives. We define precision

P_1 as $\frac{|TP|}{m}$ and recall R_1 as $\frac{|TP|}{n}$. We assess the component accuracy using the F1 score defined as

$$CA = 2 \cdot \frac{P_1 \cdot R_1}{P_1 + R_1} = 2 \cdot \frac{|TP|}{m+n} \tag{3}$$

Component Completeness. For each true positive component $C_k^D = (V_k^D, E_k^D) \in TP$ that matches a component in the reference graph $C_l^R = (V_l^R, E_l^R)$, we define the precision P_2^k as $\frac{|V_k^D \cap V_l^D|}{|V_k^D|}$ and recall R_2^k as $\frac{|V_k^D \cap V_l^D|}{|V_l^D|}$. We assess the component completeness using the averaged F1 score defined as:

$$CC = \frac{1}{|TP|} \sum_{C_i \in TP} 2 \cdot \frac{P_2^i \cdot R_2^i}{P_2^i + R_2^i} \tag{4}$$

4.3 Results

We ran a series of experiments that explored the influence of meta-parameters, embedding strategy, and log quality on the method's quality. The following subsections present detailed results.

Mapping of the Discovered Graph to the Reference Graph. The discovered graph uses tokens retrieved from the log that do not necessarily match the names of the data attributes in the reference graph. To be able to provide any metrics, we manually mapped all of the nodes in the discovered graphs to the respective nodes of the reference graph. Sometimes such mapping could not be performed as the discovered node did not have a good representation in the reference graph. Also, the node names discovered from the log were sometimes ambiguous (especially for low N values), so the mapping in such cases might not be accurate. It is worth noting that the discovered graph can be analyzed not only in comparison to the reference graph but also from the perspective of the additional business information that was retrieved from the log. Such analysis is, however, beyond the scope of this paper.

Meta-parameters. We ran over 300 experiments with the following combination of meta-parameter values:

- $N \in \{1, 2, 4\}$
- $ies \in \{0.5, 0.7, 0.9\}$
- $oes \in \{0.1, 0.2, 0.5\}$
- $mt \in \{5, 7, 10\}$
- $ml \in \{2, 3, 5, 10\}$

Figure 16 presents the average values of CA, CC, P_1, R_1 metrics for various values of N across all the experiments. It can be observed that the precision of component discovery (P_1) remains relatively high and stable across all the experiments, which can be seen in its histogram presented in Fig. 17. High values of precision show that the discovered relationships are useful (there is a low level of false positives). Similarly, we can observe that the CC metric's values are generally above 0.5 (see the histogram in Fig. 18). There is a clear area of meta-parameters for which our method does not find any data relationships, which can be seen as the zero values in both histograms. It turns out that the main contributing factor, in this case, is the high value of the oes meta-parameter (0.5) in conjunction with high values of other meta-parameters (from the high end of the tested spectrum).

Tables 5 and 6 present the two quality metrics in the context of oes and ies meta-parameters. Color intensity in both tables visualizes the achieved average quality results. The single best component accuracy was achieved for $oes = 0.2$, $ies = 0.7$, $N = 1$, $mt = 5$, $ml = 3$, and the single best component completeness was achieved for $oes = 0.5$, $ies = 0.9$, $N = 2$, $mt = 5$, $ml = 5$. We use these configurations for further experiments with embedding strategies and log quality.

Figure 19 presents an example graph discovered by our method. It can be observed that the majority of the nodes in the discovered graph are related to applications, whose logs have the highest level of business information load, coming from applications B, G, D, A (see Table 4). That confirms that the major driver of the quality of the discovered graph is the information content of a log.

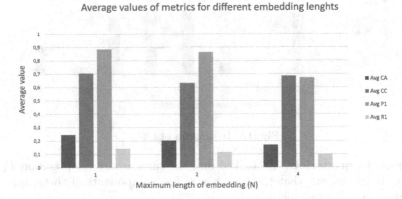

Fig. 16. Average values of the method's quality metrics for various lengths of token embeddings.

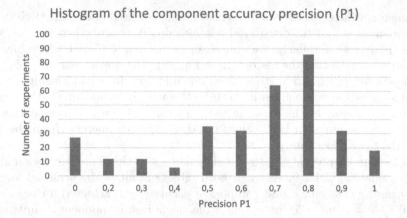

Fig. 17. Histogram of P_1.

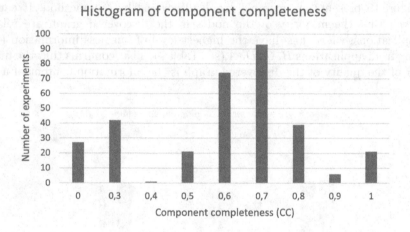

Fig. 18. Histogram of CC.

Precision Degradation. We looked into the cases where the precision P_1 was lowered. It turned out that the reason was few components of the graph, that were discovered for two reasons:

- accidental relationship caused by the low cardinality of data attribute value set (e.g. currency codes),
- not distinctive enough embedding of a token.

The first issue can be addressed by increasing the value of the ml meta-parameter which would enforce considering only longer tokens (thus with potentially higher cardinality). In practice, it turns out that while increasing ml helps with removing the accidental relationships for some tokens, it also disables the discovery of real relationships for other tokens. Tweaking the value of ml means balancing between precision and recall.

Table 5. Average value of CA in relation to *ies* and *oes* values.

ies	oes		
	0,1	0,2	0,5
0,5	0,17	0,19	0,02
0,7	0,18	0,21	0,02
0,9	0,18	0,20	0,02

Table 6. Average value of CC in relation to *ies* and *oes* values.

ies	oes		
	0,1	0,2	0,5
0,5	0,76	0,64	0,44
0,7	0,77	0,67	0,44
0,9	0,81	0,69	0,44

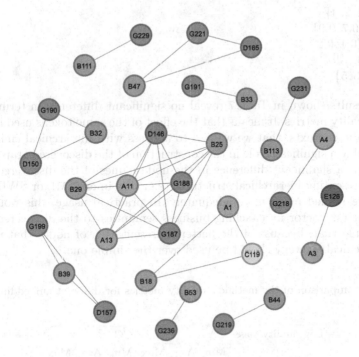

Fig. 19. Example of data attribute relationship graph discovered by our method for $oes = 0.2$, $ies = 0.7$, $N = 1$, $mt = 5$, $ml = 3$.

The latter reason is related to the specifics of the dataset. NDEASYS processes, among other data, SWIFT messages, for which it is common to use the same token in multiple contexts and multiple meanings. Due to the embedding strategy, such tokens, although semantically different, would receive the same embedding and be treated as the same data attribute. This renders unwanted components in the discovered graph.

Recall Degradation. Figure 16 shows that the recall R_1 value is much lower than the precision, which suggests that a lot of components were not discovered by our method. As the main reason for this, we see the low level of the business information load across the logs. In Table 4 it can be seen that only the logs of applications B, D, and G are rich in business information, coming mostly from logging the full content of the received events.

Embedding Strategy. The results presented above refer to the simple embedding strategy. We ran a series of experiments for the hierarchical embedding strategy within a limited scope of meta-parameters. The scope was chosen to match the area, where the simple embedding strategy rendered the best results. We used the following combination of meta-parameter values:

- $N \in \{1, 2, 4\}$
- $ies \in \{0.7, 0.9\}$
- $oes \in \{0.1, 0.2\}$
- $mt = 5$
- $ml \in \{3, 5\}$

The results shown in Table 7 reveal no significant difference in terms of the defined quality metrics. It means that the effect of the same tokens used in different semantic contexts, that we wanted to address with hierarchical embedding, does not play a significant role in the construction of the discovered graph. There is, however, a significant difference in the node names of the discovered graph. Nodes representing hierarchical structures (e.g. tags in an XML or SWIFT document) are named much more adequately. In practical usage, this would be a very important factor in attaching business semantics to the discovered nodes. We conclude that, because of the better representation of nodes that it offers, the hierarchical strategy should be used over the simple one.

Table 7. Comparison of the method's quality metrics for different embedding strategies.

Log quality class	CA			CC		
	Min	Avg	Max	Min	Avg	Max
Simple	0,17	0,22	0,28	0,65	0,74	0,85
Hierarchical	0.2	0.23	0.26	0.67	0.71	0.76

Log Quality. We expect that the quality of our method is highly dependent on the log contents. The term *log quality* refers to the level of business information load of the logs. We simulate logs of different quality by artificially removing some classes of log entries and observing their influence on the method's quality. We evaluate the following scenarios:

- Full log - full content of the log is considered,
- Technical log (3% of the full log) - only the technical entries are considered,
- Event log (10% of the full log) - only the events (detailed input received by an application) are considered.

We compared the quality metrics for different log quality classes within the same area of meta-parameter values that were used for comparing the embedding strategies. The experiments revealed that using the technical log does not bring any value. Although some graphs were discovered, their edges represented only accidental relationships corresponding to the co-occurrence of the same technical values in different logs. We conclude that technical log messages are not contributing to the discovery of data attribute relationships and should be treated as noise. In the case of our dataset, they constitute only 3% of the total log contents but for other datasets, it might be good to consider filtering them out to decrease the computation time.

Table 4 shows that most information in the event log comes from the log entries created by applications B, G, and D. Therefore, apart from comparing the discovered graphs to the original reference graph, we also compared them to the reduced reference graph constructed by retaining only the nodes owned by these applications. Table 8 presents the comparison of the method's quality metrics between different log quality classes. The results achieved between the full log and event log are very similar, especially when the reduced reference graph is used for comparison. This shows that an event log might be the most practical fragment of the log to use for analysis. With just 10% of the full log size, it allows us to achieve similar results. This is because of the high level of business information load associated with event log messages.

Table 8. Comparison of the method's quality metrics for different log quality classes.

Log quality class	Relative log size	CA			CC		
		Min	Avg	Max	Min	Avg	Max
Full log	100%	0,17	0,22	0,28	0,65	0,74	0,85
Event log	10%	0,15	0,17	0,2	0,68	0,72	0,76
Event log (reduced reference graph)	10%	0,16	0,19	0,21	0,82	0,83	0,83
Technical log	3%	0	0	0	0	0	0

Beyond the Reference Graph. The reference graph was constructed by mapping the NDEASYS specification. The nodes of the discovered graph had to be mapped to the nodes of the reference graph. As mentioned previously in the paper, some nodes could not be mapped as there was no good representative in the reference graph. A closer look into those nodes revealed that the vast majority of them reflected the technical aspects in the log (usually an accidental correlation of technical values that was transformed to an edge of the discovered graph). However, around 8% of those nodes held business meaningful terms in their embeddings, which fell into two categories:

- actual data attributes that were revealed by log analysis, but were missing from the specification (around 7% of all the unmapped nodes),
- additional business context (around 1% of all the unmapped nodes) - nodes representing descriptive log entries containing business terms.

The first category shows the potential of log analysis to reveal hidden attributes of the data model and their relationships by looking into the actual data. The second category becomes important in a real-life scenario, where no reference graph is available.

In a practical use case, there will be no reference graph and our method will face the additional challenge of translating the nodes of the discovered graph to some business terms understandable for a user. In the case of the NDEASET2 dataset, a lot of the node names come from the embeddings representing well-defined data formats (e.g. tags in XML messages described by a schema or SWIFT message tags, described by an ISO standard). However, some data attributes that are not standardized (e.g. internal data model of an application) need to be described in business terms when put in the log message. Otherwise, the node representing them will be meaningless for a user. This shows the importance of using business terms by developers to describe the values they are outputting in the log.

4.4   Suggested Logging Practices for Developers

As it stems from the presented results, for log analysis to be able to efficiently discover data relationships, a high business information load is required in the logs. Developers could support this process by using the following practices:

1. Log full details of the business events received by an application,
2. When logging data values, make sure to amend its business meaning to the log message,
3. Make technical and business log messages easily distinguishable.

All of the above recommendations are rather easy to implement and naturally used by developers for application diagnostics. Logging the full content of the input might seem problematic because of its potentially large size and performance hit caused by logging. However, in enterprise systems, it is quite common for applications to exchange data over common infrastructure (e.g. enterprise message buses). In such cases the messages passed to the message bus can be considered a pure event log and no additional inside-application logging of events is necessary.

4.5 Threats to Validity

Internal threats to validity include the construction of the NDEASET2 dataset and the level of detail of logs. We tried to mitigate both threats by choosing applications that provided a decent level of diversity. We diversified the dataset by selecting applications maintained by different teams, potentially following different logging standards. Also, the application diversity (different types of applications included in the dataset) is meant to increase the overall representativeness of the dataset. We presented the influence of log quality on the results of our method and pointed out the need for logs to be rich in business information for them to be useful.

The biggest external threat to validity is the dataset from Nordea Bank, which might not be representative of the whole bank and enterprise systems in general. This threat might come from the specific dataset that was chosen for research but also from potential formal or informal rules regarding logging practices enforced by Nordea. In the future, we will try to find other datasets to further mitigate these threats. It is worth noting that although publicly available datasets are very beneficial for the validation of our method and the general reproducibility of research, they will never be close to the size and complexity of real-life enterprise systems. Therefore, apart from selecting open-source datasets, we will seek further datasets inside Nordea Bank to retain real-world validation for our research.

Conclusion validity is threatened by data attributes with low cardinality of values (e.g. currency symbols in the banking industry). Such data attributes can be falsely considered as related just because of a high chance of them getting the same values. Another threat to conclusion validity is the low level of detail of logs, which can result in relationships between data attributes not being detected.

5   Related Work

Discovering relationships between data is a topic studied by schema matching discipline [17]. This domain is very broad and uses several techniques, including matching strings, matching words in certain languages, matching graphs, or using ontologies representing knowledge in certain fields. The goal of traditional schema matching is to match elements between two schemas given as input. The authors of [16] and [15] study a more general case where the number of schemas to be matched is greater than two. Finding similarities in attribute values (called duplicates) is the basis of the method proposed in [4]. The authors perform schema matching based on a small number of matching values in two schemas. [19] proposes a method for matching knowledge graphs. The authors split the process into schema-level and instance-level matching. In the first phase, matching is performed using only schema information, while in the second phase, the result is further refined by matching the values that schema attributes take. All of the approaches in the schema matching domain assume full knowledge of the individual schemas being matched. What is in the area of interest is only finding the correspondence between the attributes of the schemas. This is a significant difference compared to our method, which needs to discover both the schemas and their corresponding attributes.

Semantic data type discovery is a field of research that focuses on assigning types that have well-defined meanings to schema attributes. As compared to regular type detection (e.g. whether an attribute is a string, int, or boolean), semantic types hold much more information (e.g. postal code, surname, country) and as such could be used to match attributes of different schemas. [7] introduces *Sherlock*, a supervised-learning approach to semantic type detection. It uses the VisNet dataset to train a classifier that detects one of the 78 semantic types defined in the *T2Dv2Gold Standard* dataset. The authors of [20] propose the *SATO* algorithm, which extends *Sherlock* by incorporating the concept of context. Data attributes are matched not only based on the values they take but also based on the neighbor attributes in the same schema. Such an approach allows to properly classify semantic types for attributes with a low number of samples. Both [20] and [14] rely on model training for a given dataset which contrasts with the unsupervised approach we take to derive data relationships. [14] describes *RaF-STD*, an unsupervised learning approach to semantic type detection. The authors exploit triples of schema attributes that share common values and iteratively introduce higher-level virtual attributes representing the notion of similarity. This method does not require any prior knowledge of the source schemas but requires the existence of such schemas, which we do not assume in our method.

Automated log analysis is a field of research that focuses on the extraction of data from logs in an automated fashion. The authors of [10] split this field based on the type of knowledge being extracted. According to this classification, domain model extraction is a field that is somewhat relevant to data attribute discovery. [3] presents a method for discovering an ontology based on event logs and process mining techniques. The method is validated using a dataset of stack overflow posts and proved to generate a valid ontology in a computer science domain. The use of an event log requires intensive log preprocessing, which is not the case with our method, which operates on raw application logs, with very little preprocessing to unify log format across applications.

Log template generation is a field of research that aims to find patterns in lines of log files as part of a log analysis task. Typically such patterns split a log line into static and variable parts, which could be used to discover data attributes in our method. [18] and [6] are two common methods for discovering log patterns. According to [8], both of these methods do not cope well with log lines of variable length (e.g. XML document being logged), which can be a typical case of logging entry/exit data. The authors of [5] classify such log entries under the observation-point logging category and show it is one of the most common types of log entries. [8] proposes an *SLT* method for log template generation, which is well-suited for handling log entries of variable length but the result is coarse-grained - it does not provide any information on the position of the variable parts within a log line. Our method for data relationship discovery uses the context of neighbor tokens to detect data attributes, so the position of the variable tokens within a log entry is essential.

Word embedding is a sub-field of natural language processing that aims to represent words in some text corpus as multi-dimensional vectors. This corresponds to the initial phases of our method, where we perform the embedding of tokens of a log line. [12] and [13] are the two most popular methods for word embedding. For both, there is a large set of pre-trained models over text corpora in various languages. However, their usability to log analysis is limited. Firstly, they require training of the model on a particular text corpus, as the model is specific to the logs being analyzed. Secondly, the set of words in log corpora is infinite due to information like unique identifiers being commonly logged.

The method for discovering interactions between applications described in [8] shares similar ideas to the method described in this paper. It looks for rare tokens in various applications' logs and uses the findings to justify the hypothesis of the existence of a relationship between applications. The main difference between [8] and this paper is that [8] is focused on detecting the relationships between applications, while this paper focuses on detecting relationships between data attributes. For this purpose, we are looking not only at the rare but also the more frequent tokens. Discovery of a relationship of more frequent tokens (e.g. currency codes) in two applications cannot be treated as a good justification for the existence of a dependency (data exchange) between the applications. Therefore the method presented in this paper cannot be considered a generalization of the method described in [8]. These methods are rather complementary and the identification of relationships in data can be used to refine the set of interactions discovered by [8].

6   Conclusions and Future Work

In this paper, we proposed an unsupervised method for the automated discovery of data relationships in an enterprise system. We validated our method on a real-world dataset from a system running at Nordea Bank. The method proved to be a useful tool for obtaining an overview of the data processed by applications within an enterprise system. The method has successfully detected some correspondences between data attributes in different applications. Our method presents results with high precision. Our experiments revealed that the recall value is highly dependent on the quality of logs. The most effective usage of the proposed method is with event logs that capture the full input of business events received by applications. We provided a set of recommendations for developers aiming at improvement of logs which would support our method in reaching the best results.

In the future, we will extend the method to take advantage of additional information - locality of log entries, data attributes described by n-grams with higher values of n, and semantics hidden in the logging entries related to actions executed by an application. We will experiment with utilizing the logs of enterprise message buses and will compare the outcome with the results achieved in this paper. We will also combine the proposed method for data relationship discovery with the method of interaction discovery [8] to form a comprehensive approach for discovering knowledge about an enterprise system based on automated log analysis.

Acknowledgment. This paper was written in cooperation with the Nordea Bank which provided the log dataset and an overview of the systems that were subject to this study.

References

1. Gephi, the open graph viz platform. https://gephi.org. Accessed 30 Oct 2023
2. Acmeair: A nodejs implementation of the acme air sample application with extended logging., https://github.com/lkorzeni11/acmeair-nodejs. Accessed 24 Jul 2023. commitId: 59e8545c1e5264107e60706a360e0c8133aa8f9e
3. Barua, D., Rumpa, N.T., Hossen, S., Ali, M.M.: Ontology based log analysis of web servers using process mining techniques, pp. 341 – 344 (2019). https://doi.org/10.1109/ICECE.2018.8636791
4. Bilke, A., Naumann, F.: Schema matching using duplicates, pp. 69 – 80 (2005). https://doi.org/10.1109/ICDE.2005.126
5. Fu, Q., et al.: Where do developers log? an empirical study on logging practices in industry, pp. 24 – 33 (2014). https://doi.org/10.1145/2591062.2591175
6. He, P., Zhu, J., Zheng, Z., Lyu, M.R.: Drain: an online log parsing approach with fixed depth tree, pp. 33–40 (2017). https://doi.org/10.1109/ICWS.2017.13
7. Hulsebos, M., et al.: Sherlock: a deep learning approach to semantic data type detection, pp. 1500–1508 (2019). https://doi.org/10.1145/3292500.3330993
8. Korzeniowski, L., Goczyła, K.: Discovering interactions between applications with log analysis. In: Maria Ganzha, Leszek Maciaszek, M.P.D.S. (ed.) Proceedings of the 17th Conference on Computer Science and Intelligence Systems. ACSIS, vol. 30, p. 861 – 869 (2022). https://doi.org/10.15439/2022F172
9. Korzeniowski, L., Goczyła, K.: Discovering relationships between data in enterprise system using log analysis. In: Maria Ganzha, Leszek Maciaszek, M.P.D.S. (ed.) Proceedings of the 18th Conference on Computer Science and Intelligence Systems. ACSIS, vol. 35, pp. 141–150 (2023). https://doi.org/10.15439/2023F4617
10. Korzeniowski, L., Goczyla, K.: Landscape of automated log analysis: a systematic literature review and mapping study. IEEE Access **10**, 21892–21913 (2022). https://doi.org/10.1109/ACCESS.2022.3152549
11. Manning, C.D., Schütze, H., Weikurn, G.: Foundations of statistical natural language processing. SIGMOD Record **31**(3), 37–38 (2002). https://doi.org/10.1145/601858.601867
12. Mikolov, T., Chen, K., Corrado, G., Dean, J.: Efficient estimation of word representations in vector space (2013)
13. Pennington, J., Socher, R., Manning, C.D.: Glove: global vectors for word representation, pp. 1532 – 1543 (2014). https://doi.org/10.3115/v1/d14-1162

14. Piai, F., Atzeni, P., Merialdo, P., Srivastava, D.: Fine-grained semantic type discovery for heterogeneous sources using clustering. VLDB Journal **32**(2), 305–324 (2023). https://doi.org/10.1007/s00778-022-00743-3

15. Rahm, E., Peukert, E.: Holistic schema matching. In: Sakr, S., Zomaya, A. (eds.) Encyclopedia of Big Data Technologies, 1st edn. Springer, Cham (2019). https://doi.org/10.1007/978-3-319-77525-8_12

16. Rahm, E., Peukert, E.: Large-scale schema matching. In: Sakr, S., Zomaya, A. (eds.) Encyclopedia of Big Data Technologies, 1st edn. Springer, Cham (2019). https://doi.org/10.1007/978-3-319-77525-8_100191

17. Shvaiko, P., Euzenat, J.: A survey of schema-based matching approaches. In: Spaccapietra, S. (ed.) Journal on Data Semantics IV. LNCS, vol. 3730, pp. 146–171. Springer, Heidelberg (2005). https://doi.org/10.1007/11603412_5

18. Vaarandi, R., Pihelgas, M.: Logcluster - a data clustering and pattern mining algorithm for event logs, pp. 1–7 (2015). https://doi.org/10.1109/CNSM.2015.7367331

19. Xue, X., Zhu, H.: Matching knowledge graphs with compact niching evolutionary algorithm. Expert Syst. Appl. **203** (2022). https://doi.org/10.1016/j.eswa.2022.117371

20. Zhang, D., Suhara, Y., Li, J., Hulsebos, M., Demiralp, a., Tan, W.C.: Sato: Contextual semantic type detection in tables. Proc. VLDB Endowment **13**(11), 1835 – 1848 (2020). https://doi.org/10.14778/3407790.3407793

8th Workshop on Advances in Programming Languages (WAPL 2023)

Performance Analysis of Compiler Support for Parallel Evaluation of C++ Constant Expressions

Andrew Gozillon[1] , Seyed Hossein Haeri[3] , James Riordan[2] ,
and Paul Keir[2(✉)]

[1] Advanced Micro Devices AB, Nordenskioldsgatan 11 A,
Office 233, 211 19 Malmö, Sweden
andrew.gozillon@amd.com
[2] School of Computing, Engineering and Physical Sciences,
University of the West of Scotland, Paisley PA1 2BE, UK
{james.riordan,paul.keir}@uws.ac.uk
[3] University of Bergen, Norway & PLWorkz R&D, Belgium
Av. Chapelle-aux-Champs 49, Brussels, Belgium
hossein@uib.no

Abstract. Metaprogramming, the practice of writing programs that
manipulate other programs at compile-time, continues to impact software
development; enabling new approaches to optimisation, static analysis,
and reflection. Nevertheless, a challenge associated with metaprogramming techniques, including C++ *constexpr* functionality, is an increase
in compilation times. This paper presents *ClangOz*, a novel Clang-based
research compiler that addresses this issue by evaluating annotated constant expressions in parallel, thereby reducing compilation time.

By evaluating constant expressions in parallel, ClangOz significantly
reduces compilation times for metaprogramming-intensive codebases,
enhancing developer productivity and iterative software development processes. To control this, ClangOz includes novel compiler intrinsics allowing
developers to take full advantage of *constexpr* language features.

New i9-13900K benchmark results here demonstrate the performance
advantage of ClangOz over traditional compilers, including a decrease in
compile times across more benchmarks; and 100% parallel efficiency in two
cases. Also introduced here is the C'est library, which provides a subset of
the C++ standard library, with extended *constexpr* support.

We highlight applications of the *constexpr* language feature, and
emphasise the relevance of ClangOz, a compiler tailored for parallel evaluation of relevant constant expressions. Developers can now utilise modern
metaprogramming, while minimising compile times parametrically.

Keywords: Compiler · Parallelism · C++ · Partial Evaluation

1 Introduction

Compile time metaprogramming in C++ has been of interest since the discovery that C++ templates were Turing-complete [38]. Exploration of compile time

© The Author(s), under exclusive license to Springer Nature Switzerland AG 2024
A. Jarzębowicz et al. (Eds.): KKIO 2023, LNBIP 499, pp. 129–152, 2024.
https://doi.org/10.1007/978-3-031-51075-5_6

metaprogramming has resulted in the addition of constant expressions to the language; a concept proposed in 2003 [17]; and added in C++11 [21] with the inclusion of the *constexpr* specifier. A constant expression is an expression which would remain constant at runtime and could thus be evaluated at compile time. The *constexpr* specifier allows functions and variable declarations to assert that they can be evaluated at compile time. With the addition of this specifier, compile time programming has become more approachable, with a syntax almost identical to runtime code.

Since the addition of constant expressions to C++, the standard library specification has begun to incorporate support for both compile time and runtime execution for its functionality. With the increasing *constexpr* support, larger program segments can now be evaluated at compile time. However, as more components are evaluated at compile time, so too do compilation times increase. Adding parallelism to a program can help increase performance when used correctly. Yet parallelism is currently only available in runtime contexts; there is no existing concept of C++ compile time parallelism.

We here introduce ClangOz [1], an experimental Clang-based [26] compiler which adds support for the parallel execution of for-loops at compile time. ClangOz seeks to give users control of parallelism through compiler intrinsics. The intrinsics are a set of functions built into the compiler, which may be utilised to convey information about the algorithm being *constexpr*-parallelised to ClangOz. A higher level application programming interface (API) is also provided which builds upon the *execution policy* overloads of existing standard C++ runtime library functions such as *std::for_each*, to allow easier access to *constexpr* parallelism.

In this extended version of our recently published research paper [18], we introduce a new fintech benchmark; alongside an edge detection image processing benchmark built upon our prototype *constexpr* parallel implementation of the Khronos SYCL specification. All benchmarks have been executed on a recent CPU architecture; the Intel Core i9-13900K, which introduces a heterogeneous environment integrating both performance and efficiency cores. Furthermore, we discuss both the C'est library - our partial implementation of the C++ standard library, with additional *constexpr* support; as well as the ClangOz compiler timing intrinsics, underpinning the novel constant expression benchmarking showcased in our work.

A survey of related and relevant literature is presented in Sect. 2. Section 3 covers the ClangOz compiler, discussing its architecture; parallel constant expression evaluation; and intrinsics library, along with a concise implementation example of *std::for_each*. Most of our benchmarks utilise custom *constexpr* versions of C++ standard library components, and Sect. 4 discusses these aspects of our C'est library. Before concluding in Sect. 6, Sect. 5 reports on experiments, with benchmarks facilitated by the novel compile time parallelism feature, and considers performance and scaling in comparison with serial counterparts.

2   Background

Parallelism within compilers is not new, and much research has been undertaken, aiming to speed up different phases of the compiler. For example, investigation on the parallelisation of parsing [3], assembling [24], semantic analysis [31], lexical analysis [34] and code generation [19] compiler phases have been conducted. Despite this, most modern compilers avoid the additional complexity of adding parallelism for performance. The research presented in this paper differs from the prior art as it pertains to a smaller segment of the compiler; a subsection of the semantic analysis process. Nevertheless, it does adds an overhead for compiler developers; even if it is smaller in scope. This work is also distinct in placing the parallelism into the users' hands through an API, making the parallelism explicitly programmable.

The landscape of C++ compile time programming has continued to expand in recent years. In the 2020 iteration of the language (C++20 [22]) dynamic memory allocation and deallocation at compile time was added [14]. This allowed the creation of variable size containers at compile time. C++20 also introduced a feature called *Concepts* [37], allowing a user to constrain template instantiation according to composable boolean predicates. Concepts allow for increased user defined type-safety within code bases, while improving error messages. Further proposals are pending, with the most interesting possible additions being meta-classes [36] and reflection [11]. The former allows users to define a compile time function that manipulates how a class's definition is generated; for example to make member functions of a class public by default. The latter allows deeper compile time introspection of types; for instance, to check the names of class members.

Additions like these to the language specification have allowed for projects that were previously impossible. The processing of regular expressions at compile time [15], static reflection through a library rather than the language [32], big-integer computation [9] and compile time functional composition [16] are prominent examples. Such projects require a sizable amount of computation at compile time, and would benefit from acceleration by *constexpr* parallelisation.

Providing language features to allow processing at compile time is not unique to C++. Lisp [35], D [4], Rust [28], Julia [7], Elixir [29] and Circle [6] all give various compile time facilities. Lisp was the first language with Turing-complete compile time functionality; Lisp provides this feature in the form of macros which, unlike C-style macros, can perform computation as well as text substitution. The D programming language has many similarities to C++. Its compile time features are based upon it, with the intent to simplify them. The D language allows compile time programming using constructs similar to C++ templates and constant expressions, though it extends these concepts with the introduction of eponymous and nested templates. In contrast: Rust, Julia and Elixir make use of Lisp-style macros that manipulate the AST for their compile time metaprogramming. Rust and Julia also support compile time computation through constant expressions that share similarities with C++. The Circle language is interesting as it builds on-top of C++17, adding a host of new data-driven metaprogramming features including range operators and pack generators. The concepts introduced in this paper could in turn be extended to such programming languages, having similar compile time capabilities, albeit in a different guise when the capabilities are macro based.

The evaluation of constant expressions at compile time has parallels in the field of partial evaluation [23], where programs are specialised dynamically at runtime or statically at compile time to achieve better performance. Partial evaluation of programs can lead to optimisations including constant folding; code simplification; strength reduction; and control flow optimisation. All such optimisations are possible through the explicit utilisation of *constexpr* within C++ to specialise code; and we recognise that the comparison of partial evaluation and C++'s compile time features has been made before [40]. Research into partial evaluation and its applications have been ongoing for many years; and recently applied to the field of High-Performance Computing with the aim of increasing performance in a myriad of ways. For example, using static partial evaluation to optimise memory access patterns on the GPU [39]; creating domain specific languages utilising partial evaluation to facilitate high-performance libraries for accelerators [27]; and in the development of compilers and interpreters for dynamic languages that utilise partial evaluation to speculatively optimise code [41]. In a similar vein to the work in this paper for compile time evaluation, some research on parallel evaluation of partial evaluation has also been conducted. Some examples are the parallelisation of a partial evaluator utilised in the specialisation of mutually recursive procedures [12]; distributed parallelisation of partial evaluators within programming languages [33]; and parallelisation of partial evaluations within evolutionary algorithms [10].

3   Compile Time Parallelism

The ClangOz[1] compiler builds on Clang by adding parallelisation support to *for* loops in specific *constexpr* contexts. This is performed using an API of four intrinsic functions[2], used to communicate to the compiler how a loop should be parallelised. The intrinsic calls are placed within the function body containing each targeted loop; and assist with loop dependency analysis [25].

When the following constraints have been met within a *constexpr* function, ClangOz will use these intrinsics to gather the information required to partition the loop body across multiple CPU threads. There are two constraints that have to be met by a *for* loop to be *constexpr* parallelised. First, it must be within a *constexpr* function; and adjacent to the appropriate parallelisation intrinsics. Second, the enclosing function must include our new C++ execution policy class [2] within its parameter list; and be invoked with the corresponding object as an argument. An execution policy parameter allows an algorithm designer to overload a function's behaviour based on the *type* of each distinct policy. For example, a *std::for_each* function may be passed a *std::execution::parallel_policy*

---

[1] The compiler has no connection to Mozart and the Oz language.

[2] These are not *Clang* intrinsics per se; though they perform a similar role.

which indicates that the *std::for_each* should select an overload that has a parallelised implementation. In the case of ClangOz a new *constexpr_parallel_policy* was added to ClangOz's C++ standard library (a modified version of Clang's implementation of the C++ standard library: libc++) which is used to indicate that a function should be *constexpr* parallelised if possible.

These constraints define a minimal C++ API that *constexpr* functions must meet to undergo the parallelisation process. The constraints were added as a way to limit the scope at which ClangOz would try to apply its parallelisation process.

There are some limitations of the ClangOz compiler worth noting. First, there is no support for nested parallelism; only the outer loop of a loop nest is parallelisable. Second, only a single loop is parallelisable within each function. Thirdly, only container argument types owning *contiguous* data are supported; and container objects must utilise a pointer-based iterator. An example usage of a *constexpr* parallel *std::for_each* from ClangOz's modified libc++ can be found in Listing 1. *execution::ce_par* is a simple, 1-byte, pre-constructed *constexpr_parallel_policy* object. Passing this policy into the *std::for_each* indicates to use a parallel implementation of the function; if one exists. The 4th argument, a C++ lambda function, is then executed in parallel on the elements of the *std::array*.

```
constexpr auto f() {
  std::array<int, 4> arr {};
  std::for_each(execution::ce_par,
                arr.begin(), arr.end(),
                [](int &i) { i++; });
  return arr;
}
```

Listing 1: ClangOz's modified libc++ supports a new *ce_par* policy parameter, allowing users to avoid compiler intrinsics.

The parallelisation process takes place within Clang's constant expression evaluator. The constant expression evaluation executes within the frontend, usually during the semantic analysis stage; either when generating the abstract syntax tree (AST), or during later code generation.

The constant expression evaluator attempts constant folding on expressions stored in AST nodes; collapsing them into a value or values at compile time by processing the expression. The values are calculated and stored using Clang's *APValue* class. This class holds constant data of arbitrary bit-widths for several C++ value types; including *float*, *integer* and arrays.

Manipulation of *APValue* objects is pivotal to the parallelisation process, and in particular those that are *LValues*. Generally, *LValues* are locators for objects. An *LValue* can contain either the path from a complete object to its subobject; or a memory address offset. These are important as the majority of the parallelised standard C++ library algorithms use *iterators*: an idiomatic abstraction over the traversal strategy of each container. The parallelisation process manipulates and gathers information from these iterators; with pointers a common form.

Clang's *CallStackFrame* and *EvalInfo* classes are also integral. The former acts as a call stack for the constant expression evaluator; maintaining information for the current call stack frame, and tracking the arguments passed to the frame and the temporaries that reside within it. Alongside, a pointer to the preceding frame in the stack is also stored, to facilitate backwards traversal. The *EvalInfo* class maintains information about the expression being evaluated, including the *CallStackFrame*. These classes maintain most of the evaluator's state during evaluation.

Two Clang AST components that are useful for the parallelisation process are the *Expr* and *Decl* family of classes. The former maintains information about types of expressions; for example *CallExpr* maintains information about function invocations. The latter tracks declarations or definitions of different language constructs; for example information on each function definition is stored within a *FunctionDecl*.

3.1   The Parallelisation Process

The parallelisation process consists of four phases (See Fig. 1). The first phase is *verification*, confirming that the two constraints have been satisfied. These constraints are checked whenever a *for* loop is encountered within a *constexpr* context. The first step checks the enclosing context is a function, before iterating over the function's parameters to detect if the function takes a *constexpr_parallel_policy* as an argument. As nested parallelism is not supported, the second check makes sure that no other *constexpr* parallel tasks are in flight.

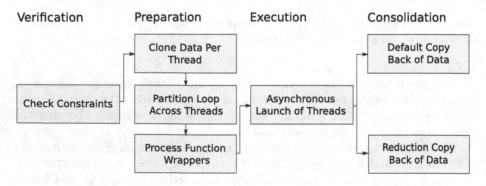

Fig. 1. Compilation Phases involved in the Parallelisation Process

The second phase is *preparation*, where the intrinsics are processed; local data is prepared for each thread; and the loop space is partitioned. This phase involves creating a clone of the *EvalInfo* object per thread, as well as each of the *CallStackFrame*s it contains. The *APValue*s that reside in each *CallStackFrame* are also cloned; representing both dynamically and statically allocated data.

After the data has been cloned the partitioning process begins, using static loop partitioning to divide the work across multiple threads. If the data cannot be divided evenly across threads which are maintained by a single thread pool; any excess work is given to the final thread. This partitioning process is part of the *LoopIntrinsicGatherer* class, an addition to ClangOz that implements the functionality for handling the intrinsics, cloning data and reducing data. The partitioning is reliant on the _ _ *BeginEndIteratorPair* or _ _ *PartitionUsingIndex* intrinsic being used by the creator of the function to specify the loop bounds. These and other intrinsics are discussed further in Sect. 3.2.

The intrinsics are discovered prior to the partitioning process by traversing the function body containing the loop, statement by statement, checking the name of each function called against the list of intrinsic names. This is done by making the *LoopIntrinsicGatherer* a child of *Clang*'s *ConstStmtVisitor* which recursively visits a *Stmt*, breaking it into its constituent *Stmt* types. Each *Stmt* in the body of the *FunctionDecl* is then iterated over, and passed to the recursive visitor, which then searches for *CallExpr* nodes to verify and process.

Each thread has copies of the variables defining the loop bounds; provided in the initialisation, condition and iteration statements. Dividing the workload across threads requires offsetting the underlying *APValue*s of these variables; and in particular those found in the loop's condition statement, which help to define its range. In the case of the standard library algorithms, the loop conditions are equality checks; for example, comparing the start and end pointers from a container to check that they are not equal. It is possible to offset the pointer's *APValue* to point to the start and end of the loop partition for each thread, effectively segmenting the loop.

To calculate the appropriate size of each partition, and the amount required to offset the loop's start and end by, the size of the iteration space must be calculated. This distance can then be divided by the number of partitions provisioned. For loop bounds defined by integer values, this is straightforward. With pointers, the size of the container's element type is required; and memory addresses to a contiguous container are traversed using an offset based on the size of the element type. Calculating the distance requires utilising this size to convert from a memory address to an integral number representing the loop's range. This can then be used to calculate the offset for each partition, and then each pointer can be offset by the appropriate amount. Only containers of contiguous data are supported, as partitioning non-contiguous data involving arbitrary memory locations is non-trivial, and time intensive.

After the work has been distributed, the third phase begins: the *execution* phase. Tasks, encapsulated as C++ function objects (often lambda functions), are launched asynchronously, and then a *wait* for completion is issued. The parallelised task contains the *constexpr* evaluation of the body of the loop. The initialisation and destruction steps in the loop's evaluation are executed sequentially, and occur once on loop entry and exit. The task itself does not deviate from the original sequential algorithm.

The final phase after thread completion is *consolidation*. This phase focuses on synchronising thread data back into the main process's *CallStackFrame* and *EvalInfo*, allowing sequential evaluation to continue. This is done in two steps, the first copies the cloned data back into its original location. The second step involves an optional reduction, and is controlled by the _ _ *ReduceVariable* intrinsic discussed in Sect. 3.2. Data that is marked for reduction by _ _ *ReduceVariable* skips the first step.

Data which has been cloned, is split into two components before being copied back. The second component is specific to array data, the first is for everything else. A primary thread is selected to copy data for the non-array component, which is dependent on an *EvalStmtResult* object returned by each parallel task. This *EvalStmtResult* is a Clang enumerator that contains different evaluation result flags for statements. Each returned *EvalStmtResult* is checked: if all return successfully, then the final thread is selected as the primary thread. As the whole loop range was iterated across, the newest values should be contained within the final partition space. In other cases, where threads complete early, perhaps due to encountering *return* or *break* statements, the first thread that signalled early completion is selected. This ensures that values in later partitions are ignored, as they would not be processed when executing the loop sequentially.

The re-synchronisation of arrays is done by determining which elements have been written to by each thread and then copying these elements from the respective clone, to the original. This does not factor in alteration of the same array element by multiple threads.

Applying reductions can be thought of as a special case of the first step which can be requested by a user through the _ _ *ReduceVariable* intrinsic when a more complex data synchronisation method is required. There are several different types of reduction possible, and these are discussed in Sect. 3.2.

3.2   The Intrinsic Functions

The compiler intrinsics are used as standard C++ functions, to communicate to the compiler how a loop is to be parallelised. They are implemented as functions rather than Clang intrinsics as it simplified modifications to the parallelisation process. This use of an API of intrinsics has much in common with OpenMP [13] and other directive-based programming paradigms.

The intrinsics required to describe the parallelisation of a loop should be placed prior to the loop within a function that meets the aforementioned constraints. There are four different intrinsic functions used for parallelisation, with descriptions listed in Table 1. The intrinsics have no body and are no-ops at runtime with a trivial overhead at compile time. They are defined as function templates so that they can be used with a variety of different types. The name of the intrinsics are prefixed with double underscores to avoid conflicts with user-defined functions. The parameters of each intrinsic allow users to pass important information to the compiler.

__ *BeginEndIteratorPair* and __ *PartitionUsingIndex* indicate to partition iterations of the loop across multiple threads based on the loop bounds indicated by their arguments. The former was designed with the use of C++ standard library containers and algorithms in mind, which make use of *begin* and *end* iterators to mark the range of loops. The latter was designed with numeric loop conditions in mind and takes an extra parameter indicating the relational operator used within the loop's condition clause.

__ *IteratorLoopStep* indicates that a pointer based index is bound to the loop's step. Clones of the index are offset by the number of loop steps taken by the loop in the thread partition at its start point. The offset is calculated by mutating the index by the number of loop steps taken by the C++ operator indicated by the *OpTy* argument. This keeps the bound value synchronised with the loop across all threads, and is used for indices not used within __ *BeginEndIteratorPair*.

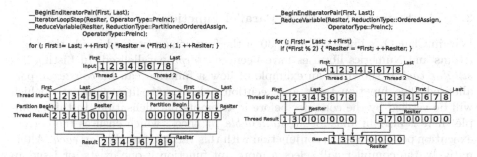

Fig. 2. Example PartitionedOrderedAssign (Left) and OrderedAssign (Right) Reduction With Two Threads

The intrinsic __ *ReduceVariable* helps to denote how a container or value should be reduced when the launched threads are joined. Three reduction types are supported: *PartitionedOrderedAssign, OrderedAssign* and *Accumulate*. *Accumulate* is used in conjunction with an accumulator variable, ensuring that the local result from each thread is combined using the specified operator to obtain a final value. *PartitionedOrderedAssign* is intended for use with containers, and its operation is illustrated on the left in Fig. 2. This reduction assigns elements to the original container in order, where each element is taken from the starting offset in each thread partition, to its final offset on thread completion. This allows appropriate collapse of data as threads are working on local copies of data rather than shared data. *OrderedAssign* (on the right of Fig. 2) is similar to *PartitionedOrderedAssign*, although it is used with containers that have not been modified in lock step with the loop. *OrderedAssign* assigns elements to the original container in order, where each element is taken from the initial offset of each cloned container to its final offset within its partition.

```
template <class _ExecutionPolicy, class _FwdIterator, class _Function>
constexpr
__enable_if_constexpr_par_execution_policy_t<_ExecutionPolicy, void>
for_each(_ExecutionPolicy&& __exec, _FwdIterator __first,
        _FwdIterator __last, _Function __f)
{
    __BeginEndIteratorPair(__first, __last);
    __ReduceVariable(__first, PartitionedOrderedAssign, PreInc);

    for (; __first != __last; ++__first)
        __f(*__first);
}
```

Listing 2: *Constexpr* parallelised libc++ *std::for_each* implementation

3.3   An Example Constexpr Parallel Function

Within ClangOz's libc++ library, 30 of the functions contained inside the Algorithms and Numerics libraries have been *constexpr* parallelised. In Listing 2 a *std::for_each* is shown as an example of how a function can be *constexpr* parallelised. The function takes an execution policy as its first parameter which will be verified by the compiler before it attempts parallelisation. In this example there is also an alias for an *std::enable_if* check, which ensures the correct execution policy is used in conjunction with this variation of *std::for_each*. Alternatively, the compiler will select a more apt function if one exists, or issue an error message.

Once the policy has been verified, each of the intrinsics is processed; and in this example there are only two. The first, _ _ *BeginEndIteratorPair* defines the loop's range which the parallelisation process uses to partition the loop across multiple threads. In this case the range is delimited by the arguments _ _*first* and _ _ *last*. The second intrinsic _ _ *ReduceVariable* states that a *PartitionedOrderedAssign* should be performed on the data pointed to by the argument _ _*first*. *OperatorType::PreInc* indicates which operator to use when traversing the data, allowing the compiler to correctly reduce the data.

4   The C'est Library

The first library dependency of most programs is included with the invoked compiler: the standard library. The C++ language and library are specified together, every few years, within each update of the C++ standard document. The latest version was ratified and published by ISO in December 2020 [22]. C++20 saw the *constexpr* specifier added to a majority of the function templates from the Algorithms and Numerics libraries; and support for these across the three main standard library distributions (libstdc++, libc++ and Microsoft STL) came quickly. Intrinsically, such function *templates* are statically polymorphic, and one can test their compile time functionality using containers which allocate their memory resources statically.

C++20 also incorporates seven proposals, a series of "relaxations of constexpr restrictions", including provision for *new-expressions* within constant expressions; so enabling the use of dynamic memory allocation within compile time calculations.

While end users could therefore then utilise pointers, and compile time dynamic memory allocation, in their own code *directly*, the feature naturally also allows the development of safer, high-level dynamically-sized containers. Such motivation is apparent in C++20's adoption of two library proposals which add support for the *constexpr* qualifier to all methods of the *std::vector* and *std::string* class templates.

All three main standard library distributions (libstdc++, libc++ and Microsoft STL), today support *constexpr* versions of the *std::vector* or *std::string* class templates. Yet real-world codes, whether executing at compile time or runtime, will expect to utilise far more than just these two containers. Consequently, we have developed C'est: an open-source, non-standard version of the C++ standard library, with enhanced support for compile time evaluation. C'est is an *incomplete* implementation of the C++20 standard library, and is utilised alongside the modified libc++ standard library provided with ClangOz. Within the *cest* namespace, the library supports useful functionality from equivalents of the standard library's *vector, string, forward_list, list, set, map, queue, deque, unique_ptr, shared_ptr* and *function*. C'est even permits IO commands to compile within constant expressions, albeit without the traditional side effects (e.g. *cest::cout « "Hello World"*). This is primarily to support execution of existing code bases within both compile time or runtime contexts.

All compile time allocations must be deallocated before the end of the containing constant expression. Consequently, as readily as the destructor of an *std::vector* or *std::string* object will deallocate the memory each owns, so will a *constexpr*-qualified declaration of either, within code capable of runtime execution, produce a compilation error. The rationale behind the term *transient* for C++20's *constexpr* memory allocation is thus apparent. It follows that the *result* of the elaborate constant expressions or programs under discussion must not itself rely on dynamic memory allocation.

5   Parallelism Benchmarking

Five *constexpr* programs based on existing benchmarks were created to test the performance of the *constexpr* parallelism implementation. The benchmarks were chosen as they have already proven to be parallelisable in a way that lends itself to the *constexpr* paralleliser. For example, complex orchestration of tasks or non-blocking tasks are not within the scope of the project; data parallelism is our focus. The benchmarks needed to be capable of being convertible to a *constexpr* program as certain features do not work at compile time, for example embedded assembly language instructions.

Two benchmarks are taken from the Princeton Application Repository for Shared-Memory Computers (PARSEC) [8]. The PARSEC suite contains several multi-threaded programs that explore different workloads on shared memory architectures. The Swaptions and BlackScholes examples were selected. Both models process financial data, however they use different methods of calculation. Swaptions makes use of Monte Carlo Simulation and BlackScholes uses a partial differential equation.

The N-Body problem and Mandelbrot benchmarks are based on existing solutions provided to The Computer Language Benchmarks Game [5]. These are micro-benchmarks with the goal of testing performance of different programming languages as opposed to directly testing parallel performance. These benchmarks are interesting in this case as they both require multiple launches of threads to attain results as opposed to the single launch of Swaptions and BlackScholes.

The final benchmark is not based on any pre-existing benchmarks, it is instead based on a program showcasing the usage of a heterogeneous parallel programming model: Khronos SYCL [20]. SYCL is a C++ programming model whcih aims to simplify programming on heterogeneous architectures through abstraction; targeting specific hardware; and hiding unnecessary complexity. In the case of the benchmark at hand, it gave the opportunity to test the feasibility of using the *constexpr* paralleliser within a larger application. The *constexpr* paralleliser replaces the underlying programming model being abstracted by SYCL facilitating a compile time parallel implementation. The SYCL benchmark performs the Sobel edge detection algorithm on an input image. It is similar to the N-Body and Mandelbrot examples as it requires multiple thread launches, however the tasks are more computationally expensive.

All benchmarks are parallelised using static partitioning. The partition sizes are selected by the compiler based on the number of threads made available and the size of each loop's range. The parallelised regions are indicated by an invocation of a *std::for_each*, which has been adapted to support *constexpr* parallelisation. The *std::for_each* invokes a function on each piece of data, in this case each thread will be given a set of data to invoke the function on individually. The *std::for_each* function is the only parallelised algorithm used within these benchmarks. It is worth noting that the main cost of the parallelisation algorithm is the cloning of data between thread partitions. Not only do the C++ iterators require cloning but so does any data used within the algorithm, such as any lambda captures, temporaries in use, or data being worked upon by the function; for example an array pointed to by the iterators.

The performance data gathered for each benchmark is displayed using two types of graph. The first is a line graph comparing serial and parallelised speed. Each of the plots in these graphs are calculated by averaging five separate runs of each of the variations of the benchmarks. The second type of graph is a speedup graph, which compares the speedup when using different numbers of threads against the ideal speedup on different problem sizes for the benchmark. The ideal speedup is a one to one match for the number of threads used. The remaining benchmark data is the difference in performance between the serial and parallel data sets. An additional speedup graph that plots the speedups for all of the benchmarks is also included to allow a holistic analysis.

5.1   Timing Compile Time Performance

Performance of the *constexpr* paralleliser is measured by comparing the speed of the parallelised constant expression evaluator against the original serial implementation on each of the benchmarks. The benchmarks are tested with different numbers of threads using an Intel Core i9-13900K CPU, containing 8 *performance cores*, with support for 16 hardware threads via hyper-threading; and 16 *efficient cores*. The base/max turbo frequencies of the effiency and performance cores respectively are 2.20 GHz/4.30 GHz and 3.00 GHz/5.40 GHz. The benchmarks were run under Ubuntu 23.10; and executed using two, four, eight and sixteen threads.

Time is measured from the beginning of a parallel region to the end of a parallel region. Rather than timing the length of the entire program, this is to measure only the regions of interest. The same location is measured for the serial execution. As stock Clang does not have any mechanism to measure or record times during constant evaluation, three intrinsics were developed within ClangOz to facilitate such benchmarking: _ _ *GetTimeStampStart()*, _ _ *GetTimeStampEnd()*, and _ _ *PrintTimeStamp()*.

```
constexpr void timing_example()
{
  std::array<int, N> id_range{};

  __GetTimeStampStart();
  std::iota(execution::ce_par, id_range.begin(), id_range.end(), 0);
  __GetTimeStampEnd();

  __PrintTimeStamp();
}
```

Listing 3: Timing a parallel *std::iota* call using ClangOz compiler intrinsics

_ _ *GetTimeStampStart()* stores an initial time point/stamp within the compiler when the *constexpr* evaluator passes through it; its partner, _ _ *GetTimeStampEnd()*, stores a second time stamp, delimiting the region of interest in time. The third intrinsic, _ _ *PrintTimeStamp()*, calculates the difference between the two time stamps, and prints it to the console's standard output. This simple interface of compiler timing intrinsics is flexible, and entirely suited to the domain. Unlike benchmark systems which relate to template metaprogramming [30], we are not here concerned specifically with C++ template instantiation; instead we proceed, as with most *constexpr* software development, in much the same way as we would when developing a program for runtime execution. In the example shown in Listing 3, the user has decided to measure the parallel constant evaluation of *std::iota*; but not the time to create the *std::array*.

It is worth noting that the same compiler is used for both the parallel and serial tests, as the intrinsics are needed for timing alongside a modified standard library implementation. This has a minor impact on the measurements for both implementations as the timing functionality requires checking the intrinsics' names, every time a function is considered for parallel execution. To determine if the parallel code path should be executed within the compiler, the verification phase discussed in Sect. 3.1 must be processed, which also adds an extra performance cost when evaluating the original serial implementation.

5.2   Mandelbrot

The Mandelbrot benchmark consists of three main areas of computation that are executed in parallel using *std::for_each*. Two initialisation steps populate a 2D array of complex values (a class containing two 64-bit floats) per pixel. Subsequently, the main Mandelbrot computation uses the naïve escape time algorithm. This algorithm loops over each complex value and performs a repeating calculation until an escape condition is met (limited to a maximum of 128 iterations). The final value generated after the escape condition has been met is the colour of the pixel which is assigned to an array of integers representing the final image.

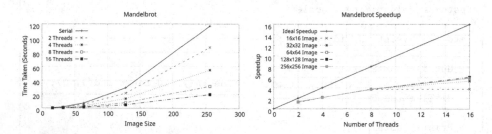

Fig. 3. Compilation Times and Speedups for the Mandelbrot Benchmark

The graphs in Fig. 3 show that the increase in data size gradually progresses towards higher polynomial growth as the number of threads diminish. With more threads, the increase in data size has less impact on compilation time. Breaking the computation into two separate parallel regions, requiring two thread group launches, has had minimal impact on this benchmark. The speedup graph shows that across all image sizes the performance improvement is similar.

5.3   BlackScholes

BlackScholes has two areas of computation which are parallelised, requiring two separate calls to *std::for_each*. The first is the main computation which computes the Black-Scholes equation; the second verifies the results from the first computation. The main data that requires cloning in this benchmark is a 1D array containing a structure for each input that owns 9 floating-point values; parsed from an external header data file using a *#include* preprocessor macro.

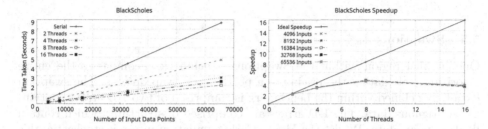

Fig. 4. Compilation Times and Speedups for the BlackScholes Benchmark

The BlackScholes data in Fig. 4 shows promising performance increases when utilising both two and four threads, but begins to wane with larger thread counts. The speedup graph on the right shows a striking fall in the speedup value for all data sizes, as the thread count moves from eight to sixteen. A possible explanation here is that hyper-threads are being used on the eight performance cores, and the execution units on each core are already maximised.

5.4   N-Body

The N-Body benchmark has two parallel regions: the advance of the particle system; and the position and velocity update. This means with more iterations of the system, more launches of threads occur. To allow a range of body counts, the number of iterations is restricted to 32; while still avoiding compilation limits. The main data cloned within the benchmark are the body attributes: structures containing seven 64-bit floats stored contiguously within an array. The number of bodies is the parameter that is varied within this benchmark.

The graphs in Fig. 5 show that increasing the number of threads again outperforms the serial implementation, thought eight threads is the closest to the ideal speedup achieved within this benchmark, with larger body numbers also aligned with better performance. This is likely due to the cost of cloning having an adverse impact on smaller workloads. As with the BlackScholes benchmark, there is no improvement in speedup as the number of cores is increased from eight to sixteen (again likely due to hyper-threading's limitations).

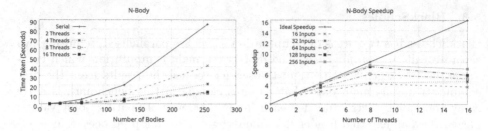

Fig. 5. Compilation Times and Speedups for the N-Body Benchmark

5.5 Swaptions

One parallel region within the Swaptions benchmark encompasses the entire algorithm, calculating the pricing of a portfolio of swap options. The swaption data being cloned within the benchmark is comprised of two 1-D arrays containing contiguous data. The 1-D arrays are comprised of structures, which contain floating point data. Whilst the Monte Carlo simulation in use is stochastic, this implementation uses a fixed seed for the random number generation.

The performance of this benchmark is linear, both in the number of swaptions, and the number of trials; with the number of swaptions varied across the different benchmark runs. In our *prior* evaluation of this benchmark, we were compelled to use a value of 2000 for the number of trials; a configuration which unfortunately forced us to vary across a relatively small number of swaptions for the performance analysis; with extremely long compilation times ceding to Clang's hard limits on constant evaluation step counts. Attempts to use smaller iteration counts for the accumulation stage, corresponding to a lower number of trials, led to a handful of problematic arithmetic operations involving NaN ("Not a Number") values. While these are ignored by default during *runtime* execution of this benchmark, arithmetic involving NaNs leads to a compilation error during constant evaluation. We have since been able to modify the benchmark. The creation of each NaN is not of itself a problem, and so we now simply identify when one is created, and avoid performing any arithmetic on it. This has allowed us to investigate a far greater number of swaptions in the current performance analysis.

The swaptions are evenly partitioned across the threads and are the locus of computation. It can be seen in Fig. 6 that as the number of swaptions can now be perfectly divided across the threads, performance is good; with the speedup graph scaling close to the ideal, at least until the stable point of eight threads. Adding eight more threads, again likely via the hyper-threading of eight performance cores, adds little benefit.

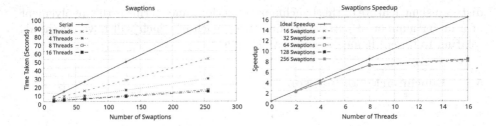

Fig. 6. Compilation Times and Speedups for the Swaptions Benchmark

5.6   SYCL Edge Detection

The SYCL benchmark is broken up into five areas of parallelism, each hidden behind the SYCL API's *parallel_for* construct; itself implemented upon our *constexpr* parallel *std::for_each*. Nesting the *std::for_each* comes at a cost, as it lies several layers down the function call stack every time threads are launched. This is a problem as the parallelisation process has to expend resources cloning each call stack frame above the *std::for_each* for each thread. This is required even if data from the prior frames is unused, albeit in this case the cloned call stack frame is empty. A further cost is the cloning of C++ lambda functions, which define the tasks to be executed within the SYCL programming model. Each area of parallelism computes a component of the final output, performing the convolution and filter application on the input image. The data that requires cloning in this benchmark are two 1-D arrays containing unsigned integers which are contained within another SYCL construct.

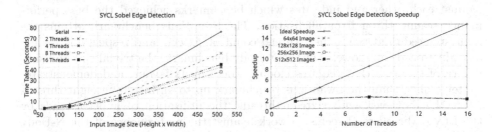

Fig. 7. Compilation Times and Speedups for the SYCL Edge Detection Benchmark

The data in Fig. 7 shows that over-subscription of threads has diminishing returns, decreasing the performance past a perfect fit. However, over-subscription still outperforms under-subscription and serial performance. Alongside the diminishing returns, the speed-up across all image sizes is similar. The extra call stack depth and cost of cloning the lambdas and their captures are likely the cause for the diminishing returns at larger thread counts; and generating threads that are not being instantly utilised comes at a greater cost. A distinguishing feature of this benchmark in performance terms is the involvement of a larger number of parallel regions (five); each of which will have overheads relating to thread launches, and data cloning.

5.7　Benchmark Comparison

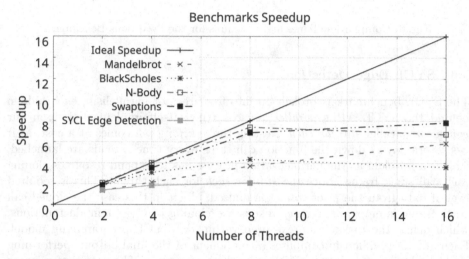

Fig. 8. Speedup Graph Comparison of all Benchmark Compilation Times

The speedup graph in Fig. 8 compares the largest variations of each benchmark against each other and indicates which benchmarks achieved the best performance scaling through parallelisation. The Swaptions benchmark attains the highest speedup at the highest thread count of sixteen; and respectable scaling at eight threads and lower. For the N-Body benchmark, the trivial size and simplicity of the data that requires cloning works in its favour, and demonstrates better scaling than the Swaptions benchmark up to an including eight threads After that however, with sixteen threads, the utilisation of hyper-threads by the LLVM thread pool seems to work against the performance of the N-Body benchmark; yet notice the *super-linear speedup* value at two and four threads. Until eight threads, the Mandelbrot benchmark is farther from the ideal speedup than BlackScholes; possibly according to the greater number of parallel regions, compared to most other benchmarks. Two of its parallel regions execute relatively small computations, to fill small arrays of data, while cloning a significant amount within the context of each parallel function call. The possibility of multiple thread launches causing cloning to have a negative impact is highlighted by BlackScholes performing better than the SYCL Edge Detection program, despite having a similar amount of data to clone per parallel region, but less parallel regions overall. With sixteen threads, hyperthreading should allow two threads to run efficiently on each of the eight performance cores, but only the

Mandelbrot and Swaptions benchmarks show a reduction in execution time at the largest thread count. The SYCL Edge Detection benchmark is distinguished by it poor scaling. While more cores always corresponds to a slight improvement in its absolute performance, when the amount of cores is accounted for, as in the speedup data, the scaling curve appears almost flat. In this regard, that the Edge Detection benchmark involves five distinct parallel regions (timed in aggregate), is likely the most noteworthy characteristic.

The results indicate that the parallelisation of *for* loops during compile time evaluation can lead to notable speedups when a large portion of the program conforms reasonably to a loop. However, the cost of cloning and partitioning data comes with significant costs. It is plausible that performance could be increased by removing the need for cloning in cases where it should not be required. For example, containers like *std::vector* or *std::array* which have no conflicting data accesses across threads should not require cloning. This could yield a performance increase in most of these benchmarks as the main input data is generally stored in such contiguous containers. Data that is not required for the execution of the parallel *constexpr* function could also be elided from the cloning process, which could have a large impact on benchmarks that contain a significant amount of data unrelated to the parallel invocation. A simple form of workload balancing may also yield reasonable results in certain circumstances where the majority of the work is not perfectly divisible by the number of threads in use. Whilst this is not seen in the performance analysis within the paper, there is likely an opportunity for improvement over the current implementation that could allow a performance increase.

6   Conclusion

As the C++ standard has evolved, additional compile time language features have been added, extending the reach of compile time metaprogramming. As C++'s compile time repertoire and use has expanded, the problem of increasing compilation times becomes prominent, leading to adverse effects on programmer work flow. This opens up the question of how to alleviate the issue. In the project introduced here, the option of acceleration through multi-threaded data-parallelism, within the compiler is investigated. ClangOz, an extended Clang compiler for C++ is introduced that can parallelise *for* loops at compile time; including with reduction/accumulation. Therein, intrinsic functions allow users to explicitly relay information to the compiler about the loop being parallelised. This firstly allows users the flexibility to implement their own low-level compile time parallel algorithms, while understanding the intrinsics' semantics. Together, the compiler and intrinsics create a framework for accelerating constant expression evaluation.

This low-level functionality has then been utilised to provide a *high-level API*, which builds on recent C++ standard library support for parallelism to implement 30 *constexpr* parallel function templates. These functions are based on existing function template signatures within the C++ standard library, and differ only by a single idiomatic argument; the policy parameter, providing access to parallelism through C++ overloading. Five compile time benchmarks were implemented that utilise a *constexpr* parallel *std::for_each* from this extended library. Through testing of these benchmarks it was shown that the ClangOz framework can have large performance benefits; with up to 100% parallel efficiency on the N-Body benchmark, and above 50% on average across the suite. These benchmarks also show that the complexity of the framework can be hidden within a library; shielding users from the onus of understanding low-level compiler intrinsics, while maintaining high performance. Benchmark results nevertheless indicate that there is still room for improvement.

The current parallelisation process has some areas that could be addressed to improve performance. One issue stems from the fact that the data copying process required when forking and joining threads can be expensive. This leads to significant startup costs, meaning that multiple sequential parallel regions for trivial amounts of computation are slower than if done sequentially. Large data dependencies can also have an impact on how much of a performance increase can be obtained from the parallelisation process. Optimising or removing the need for the cloning process would likely improve performance. Another issue is the lack of work load balancing in the implementation, which necessitates that users must choose their thread partitioning carefully. When data is indivisible by the thread count this can have a performance penalty as one thread will keep the others waiting as it deals with the excess data. A solution would be implementing a work load balancing algorithm within the compiler. These adjustments to the compiler could improve the parallelisation algorithm's overall performance.

Acknowledgements. The authors wish to thank the Royal Society of Edinburgh for their support through the Saltire International Collaboration Award (Grant Number 1981).

A   Intrinsic Functions Table

Table 1. The ClangOz Intrinsic Functions

```
template <class T, class U>
constexpr void __BeginEndIteratorPair(T& Begin, U& End);
```

Indicates the range of a *for* loop, allowing the partitioning process to split work across multiple threads. The *__BeginEndIteratorPair* or *__PartitionUsingIndex* intrinsic are required and the minimum necessary for parallelisation.

Table 1. Continued

- **Begin, End**: Indicates the beginning and end of the loop's range.
- **Type requirements**: T and U must be pointers; or single member iterators where the member is a pointer.

```
template <class T, class U>
constexpr void __PartitionUsingIndex(T LHS, U RHS, RelationalType RelTy);
```

Indicates the range of a *for* loop, allowing the partitioning process to split work across multiple threads. The _ _ *BeginEndIteratorPair* or _ _ *PartitionUsingIndex* intrinsic are required and the minimum necessary for parallelisation.

- **LHS, RHS**: Indicates the beginning and end of the loop's range.
- **RelTy**: Indicates the relational operator used within the loop's condition e.g. $>, <, !=, <=, >=$.
- **Type requirements**: T and U must be a numeric type, such as an integer.

```
template <class T>
constexpr void
__IteratorLoopStep(T& StartIter, OperatorType OpTy, const T& BoundIter);
```

States *StartIter* is bound to the loops step. Thread clones will initially be offset by invoking operator based mutation the same number of steps taken by the thread partitions loop at its start point. The operator used for mutation is indicated by *OpTy*.

- **StartIter**: Indicates the variable that will be offset.
- **OpTy**: Indicates the prefix or postfix operator (e.g. $++$) used for mutation.
- **BoundIter**: Indicates the boundary of *StartIter* if one exists, preventing offsetting past the boundary.
- **Type requirements**: T must be a pointer; or a single member iterator where the member is a pointer.

Table 1. Continued

```
template <class T>
constexpr void
__ReduceVariable(T Var, ReductionType RedTy, OperatorType OpTy);
```

Indicates that a container or value should be reduced when the launched threads are joined. Three types of reduction are supported *Partitione-dOrderedAssign*, *OrderedAssign* or *Accumulate*.

– **Var**: Notates the variable that should be reduced on thread completion.

– **RedTy**: Indicates the reduction method to be used by the compiler.

– **OpTy**: States the operator, if any, used to mutate the variable in the reduction step.

– **Type requirements**: T must be a vector or array iterator or numeric value.

References

1. ClangOz (2023). https://github.com/agozillon/ClangOz
2. Technical specification for C++ extensions for parallelism. Technical report (2018)
3. Alblas, H., op den Akker, R., Luttighuis, P.O., Sikkel, K.: A bibliography on parallel parsing. ACM SIGPLAN Not. **29**(1), 54–65 (1994). https://doi.org/10.1145/181577.181586
4. Alexandrescu, A.: The D Programming Language. Addison-Wesley Professional, Boston (2010)
5. Bagley, D.: The computer language benchmarks game (2001). https://benchmarksgame-team.pages.debian.net/benchmarksgame/
6. Baxter, S.: Circle: The C++ Automation Language (2020). https://github.com/seanbaxter/circle
7. Bezanson, J., Edelman, A., Karpinski, S., Shah, V.B.: Julia: a fresh approach to numerical computing. SIAM Rev. **59**(1), 65–98 (2017). https://doi.org/10.1137/141000671
8. Bienia, C., Kumar, S., Singh, J.P., Li, K.: The parsec benchmark suite: characterization and architectural implications. In: Proceedings of the 17th International Conference on Parallel Architectures and Compilation Techniques, pp. 72–81 (2008). https://doi.org/10.1145/1454115.1454128
9. Bouman, N.J.: Multiprecision arithmetic for cryptology in C++ - compile-time computations and beating the performance of hand-optimized assembly at runtime. arXiv:1804.07236 (2018). https://arxiv.org/abs/1804.07236
10. Bouter, A., Alderliesten, T., Bel, A., Witteveen, C., Bosman, P.A.: Large-scale parallelization of partial evaluations in evolutionary algorithms for real-world problems. In: Proceedings of the Genetic and Evolutionary Computation Conference, pp. 1199–1206 (2018)

11. Chochlík, M., Naumann, A., Sankel, D.: Static reflection (2017). http://www.open-std.org/jtc1/sc22/wg21/docs/papers/2018/p0707r3.pdf
12. Consel, C., Danvy, O.: Partial evaluation in parallel. LISP Symb. Comput. **5**(4), 327–342 (1993)
13. Dagum, L., Menon, R.: OpenMP: an industry standard API for shared-memory programming. IEEE Comput. Sci. Eng. **5**(1), 46–55 (1998). https://doi.org/10.1109/99.660313
14. Dimov, P., Dionne, L., Ranns, N., Smith, R., Vandevoorde, D.: More constexpr containers (2019). http://www.open-std.org/jtc1/sc22/wg21/docs/papers/2019/p0784r7.html
15. Dusíková, H.: Compile time regular expressions (2016). https://github.com/hanickadot/compile-time-regular-expressions
16. Fahller, B.: Lift (2017). https://github.com/rollbear/lift
17. Gabriel, D.R., Stroustrup, B., Maurer, J.: Generalized constant expressions-revision 5. Technical report, ISO SC22 WG21 TR (2007)
18. Gozillon, A., Haeri, H., Riordan, J., Keir, P.: Compiler support for parallel evaluation of C++ constant expressions. In: Ganzha, M., Maciaszek, L., Paprzycki, M., Ślęzak, D. (eds.) Proceedings of the 18th Conference on Computer Science and Intelligence Systems. Annals of Computer Science and Information Systems, vol. 35, p. 481–490. IEEE (2023). https://doi.org/10.15439/2023B4268
19. Gross, T., Sobel, A., Zolg, M.: Parallel compilation for a parallel machine. In: Proceedings of the ACM SIGPLAN 1989 Conference on Programming Language Design and Implementation, pp. 91–100 (1989). https://doi.org/10.1145/73141.74826
20. Group, T.K.: Sycl 1.2.1 specification (2019). https://www.khronos.org/registry/SYCL/specs/sycl-1.2.1.pdf
21. ISO/IEC JTC 1/SC 22: ISO/IEC 14882:2011 Programming languages - C++
22. ISO/IEC JTC 1/SC 22: ISO/IEC 14882:2020 Programming languages - C++
23. Jones, N.D.: An introduction to partial evaluation. ACM Comput. Surv. (CSUR) **28**(3), 480–503 (1996)
24. Katseff, H.P.: Using data partitioning to implement a parallel assembler. In: Proceedings of the ACM/SIGPLAN Conference on Parallel Programming: Experience with Applications, Languages and Systems, pp. 66–76 (1988). https://doi.org/10.1145/62115.62123
25. Kennedy, K., Allen, J.R.: Optimizing Compilers for Modern Architectures: A Dependence-Based Approach. Morgan Kaufmann Publishers Inc., Burlington (2001)
26. Lattner, C.: LLVM and Clang: next generation compiler technology. In: The BSD Conference, vol. 5 (2008)
27. Leißa, R., et al.: AnyDSL: a partial evaluation framework for programming high-performance libraries. Proc. ACM Program. Lang. **2**(OOPSLA), 1–30 (2018)
28. Matsakis, N.D., Klock, F.S.: The rust language. ACM SIGAda Ada Lett. **34**(3), 103–104 (2014). https://doi.org/10.1145/2692956.2663188
29. McCord, C.: Metaprogramming Elixir, 1st edn. Pragmatic Bookshelf, Raleigh (2015)
30. Penuchot, J., Falcou, J.: ctbench - compile-time benchmarking and analysis. J. Open Source Softw. **8**(88), 5165 (2023). https://doi.org/10.21105/joss.05165
31. Seshadri, V., Weber, S., Wortman, D., Yu, C., Small, I.: Semantic analysis in a concurrent compiler. In: Proceedings of the ACM SIGPLAN 1988 Conference on Programming Language Design and Implementation, pp. 233–240 (1988). https://doi.org/10.1145/53990.54013

32. Sánchez, M.: tinyrefl (2018). https://github.com/Manu343726/tinyrefl
33. Sperber, M., Thiemann, P., Klaeren, H.: Distributed partial evaluation. In: Proceedings of the Second International Symposium on Parallel Symbolic Computation, pp. 80–87 (1997)
34. Srikanth, G.U.: Parallel lexical analyzer on the cell processor. In: 2010 Fourth International Conference on Secure Software Integration and Reliability Improvement Companion, pp. 28–29. IEEE (2010). https://doi.org/10.1109/SSIRI-C.2010.16
35. Steele, G.: Common LISP: The Language. Elsevier, Amsterdam (1990)
36. Sutter, H.: Metaclasses: Generative C++ (2018). http://www.open-std.org/jtc1/sc22/wg21/docs/papers/2018/p0707r3.pdf
37. Sutton, A.: C++ extensions for concepts (2017). http://www.open-std.org/jtc1/sc22/wg21/docs/papers/2017/p0734r0.pdf
38. Todd, L.V.: C++ templates are turing complete (2003). https://citeseer.ist.psu.edu/581150.html
39. Tyurin, A., Berezun, D., Grigorev, S.: Optimizing GPU programs by partial evaluation. In: Proceedings of the 25th ACM SIGPLAN Symposium on Principles and Practice of Parallel Programming, pp. 431–432 (2020)
40. Veldhuizen, T.L.: C++ templates as partial evaluation. arXiv preprint cs/9810010 (1998)
41. Würthinger, T., et al.: Practical partial evaluation for high-performance dynamic language runtimes. In: Proceedings of the 38th ACM SIGPLAN Conference on Programming Language Design and Implementation, pp. 662–676 (2017)

Author Index

A. Jarzębowicz et al. (Eds.): KKIO 2023, LNBIP 499, p. 153, 2024.
https://doi.org/10.1007/978-3-031-51075-5

Printed in the United States
by Baker & Taylor Publisher Services